DANNY PROULX'S **CABINET DOORS AND DRAWERS**

  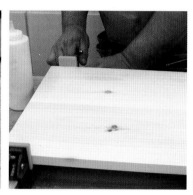 

A COMPREHENSIVE "HOW-TO" GUIDE

POPULAR WOODWORKING BOOKS
CINCINNATI, OHIO
www.popularwoodworking.com

Danny Proulx's Cabinet Doors and Drawers. Copyright © 2005 by Danny Proulx. Printed and bound in China. All rights reserved. No part of this book may be reproduced in any form or by any electronic or mechanical means including information storage and retrieval systems without permission in writing from the publisher, except by a reviewer, who may quote brief passages in a review. Published by Popular Woodworking Books, an imprint of F&W Publications, Inc., 4700 East Galbraith Road, Cincinnati, Ohio, 45236. First edition.

Visit our Web site at www.popularwoodworking.com for information on more resources for woodworkers.

Other fine Popular Woodworking Books are available from your local bookstore or direct from the publisher.

09   08   07   06   05   5   4   3   2   1

Library of Congress Cataloging-in-Publication Data

Proulx, Danny, 1947-
    Danny Proulx's cabinet doors and drawers.-- 1st ed.
        p.   cm.
    ISBN 1-55870-739-5 (alk. paper)
    1. Cabinetwork.   2. Doors.   I. Title: Cabinet doors and drawers.   II. Title.
TT197.P75962   2005
684.1'6--dc22   2004060056

ACQUISITIONS EDITOR: Jim Stack
EDITOR: Amy Hattersley
DESIGNER: Brian Roeth
LAYOUT ARTIST: Kathy Gardner
PRODUCTION COORDINATOR: Jennifer Wagner
PHOTOGRAPHER: Danny Proulx
PHOTOGRAGHIC CONSULTANT:
    Michael Bowie, Lux Photographic Services
COMPUTER ILLUSTRATOR:
    Len Churchill, Lenmark Communications Ltd.
WORKSHOP SITE PROVIDED BY: Rideau Cabinets

F+W PUBLICATIONS, INC.

READ THIS IMPORTANT SAFETY NOTICE

METRIC CONVERSION CHART

TO CONVERT	TO	MULTIPLY BY
Inches	Centimeters	2.54
Centimeters	Inches	0.4
Feet	Centimeters	30.5
Centimeters	Feet	0.03
Yards	Meters	0.9
Meters	Yards	1.1
Sq. Inches	Sq. Centimeters	6.45
Sq. Centimeters	Sq. Inches	0.16
Sq. Feet	Sq. Meters	0.09
Sq. Meters	Sq. Feet	10.8
Sq. Yards	Sq. Meters	0.8
Sq. Meters	Sq. Yards	1.2
Pounds	Kilograms	0.45
Kilograms	Pounds	2.2
Ounces	Grams	28.4
Grams	Ounces	0.035

ABOUT THE AUTHOR

Danny Proulx is the owner of Rideau Cabinets and is a contributing editor for CabinetMaker magazine. He also contributes freelance articles for *Canadian Woodworking, Canadian Home Workshop, Popular Woodworking* and other magazines. His books include *Build Your Own Kitchen Cabinets, How to Build Classic Garden Furniture, Smart Shelving and Storage Solutions, Fast and Easy Techniques for Building Modern Cabinetry, Building More Classic Garden Furniture, Building Cabinet Doors and Drawers, Build Your Own Home Office Furniture, Display Cases You Can Build, Building Frameless Kitchen Cabinets, Building Woodshop Workstations, The Pocket Hole Drilling Jig Project Book,* and *Danny Proulx's Toolboxes and Workbenches.*

Danny's Web site address is www.cabinetmaking.com and he can be reached by e-mail at danny@cabinetmaking.com.

ACKNOWLEDGEMENTS

This is another book of projects that I've enjoyed building, but I never could have accomplished it alone. The people close to me are, as always, a big part of this book. My wife Gale is constantly helpful and supportive, as is my father-in-law and assistant, Jack Chaters.

Michael Bowie of Lux Photography is the person I rely on for photographic expertise. He advises and guides me as I shoot the digital photos for each project. His concern to produce the best possible results contributed greatly to the final product.

Len Churchill of Lenmark Communications is the talented illustrator who produced the amazing project drawings. He is one of the best illustrators in the business and has an impressive understanding of the woodworking projects he's asked to draw.

As always, the Popular Woodworking Books staff continues to be unbelievably supportive. It's a team with great depth and knowledge; editor Jim Stack, Amy Hattersley, Brian Roeth and so many others are a part of every page in this book.

Luc Rousseau, a talented woodworker and cabinetmaker, has assisted me while building all the projects in this book. I also appreciate his help with other necessary — but not very glamorous — tasks around my shop.

TECHNICAL SUPPORT

A number of companies are major players in the creation of my books. They are always helpful and are valuable sources of information, supplies and advice. I've listed them in the back of this book under the heading of Suppliers. I'd appreciate your support of these fine companies.

I would like to offer special thanks to two companies who have been very supportive in producing this book: General & General International for their great woodworking machines and LRH Enterprises, Inc. for their technical support and high quality router bits, as well as the table saw molding head cutter, the "Magic Molder."

CONTENTS

INTRODUCTION

This book, as the title implies, is all about building your own cabinet doors and drawers. I'll describe as many door-construction options as possible, explain the joinery techniques, review the hardware and go over many of the possible drawer-making procedures that you might use for your cabinet projects.

The first chapter will discuss and illustrate joinery techniques, their applications and various ways to cut the same type of joint. I'll show you several methods so you can pick the one that works best for you. Drawers and doors can be constructed with a number of different joints, so I'll also show you joinery options for each application. There isn't a "right" or perfect joint for any particular situation; again, you can decide which one you like most.

Chapter two is devoted to some of the door and drawer hardware that's available. Drawer slides and hidden hinges are explained; styles as well as installation instructions are included.

Chapters three through eight deal with different door-construction methods. There are many "Shop Talk" sections that explain the various techniques, jigs and procedures needed when building doors.

You'll find out how to build a pattern-routing jig that can be used to cut decorative patterns or inlay grooves. You'll also find tips for increasing the safety of potentially dangerous woodworking procedures such as router work. Safety must be your number one concern in the shop!

Chapter nine is all about building and installing drawers. There are dozens of ways to build cabinet drawers, and I've attempted to show you as many as possible. Detailed calculations and formulas are provided so you can accurately build great drawer boxes with assurance that they will fit every time.

Chapter ten is about inlay work and the beautiful results that can be achieved using the pattern-routing jig. You'll find that inlaid doors are unique and strikingly beautiful. Everyone will want to know how you made them!

The final chapter is a review, dealing with some of the issues and techniques discussed in the book. There are also step-by-step instructions for building an adjustable router-table fence.

I hope you find this book useful and have as much fun building some of these doors and drawers as I had writing about and producing them.

Joinery Terminology and Techniques

Joining pieces of wood to form a strong connection is the central theme of woodworking. That's what it's all about — joining sticks in a prescribed way so they will remain together for years into the future. Sometimes our plans go wrong and the joint fails. Did we use the right joint for the application? Was it formed properly? Are we working to proper tolerances for the conditions our furniture project will be subjected to?

There are numerous joints that we'll use in this book to build doors and drawers. They include the butt, miter, lap, rabbet, groove, dado, mortise-and-tenon, dovetail and finger joints. Many of these joints have strange-sounding names and appear difficult to make; but when you get down to the basics of each joint, you'll discover that they are relatively simple to build with a few tools.

Shear, racking, compression and tension are all forms of stress that act on joints. It's wise to know which forces may affect your joinery, because some act to a greater degree depending on the application.

Shear is the type of force that causes pieces of a joint to slide apart. For example, a butt joint used to join boards at right angles, such as in a bookcase, will experience downward shearing pressure when weight (such as a load of books) is applied. *Racking* is a twisting force commonly applied to doors, drawers and cabinetry. Such a force can throw doors and cabinets out of square, causing binding and joint failure. *Compression* pushes a joint together, while tension tries to pull joints apart. One or more of these forces eventually affects all joints.

Wood is an organic material. It will expand and contract even after the tree it came from has been cut, milled and dried. Varying humidity levels can cause wood cells to alternately absorb and give off moisture, resulting in movement within a joint. Because, in many instances, joints are fashioned by attaching wood pieces at an angle and the grain direction and pattern of each piece is different, movement will occur at an uneven rate. A typical example is the raised panel in a frame-and-panel door. To avoid having the inevitable expansion spread the stile-and-rail joints apart, the panel is left to "float" in the door frame with a little extra space around it.

In this chapter you'll see many of the joints you can choose when building doors and drawers. I'll explain their uses and outline the exact steps required to build each of them as they appear in subsequent chapters.

BUTT JOINTS

The butt joint is simple to put together because it requires nothing except two straight-cut boards. Its strength depends on only the glue and mechanical fasteners used to secure the boards.

Butt joints are often reinforced with biscuits, splines or dowels. However, most of the glued-up raised panels for doors are simply edge-glued and are dependent on properly surfaced edges to maximize board contact.

Another common application for the butt joint is drawer making. Wood drawers have glued and nailed joints, while particleboard (PB) drawers depend entirely on screwed butt joints.

MITER JOINTS

The miter joint is a form of the butt joint. But because each piece of wood is cut at an angle, the available glue surface is increased. Therefore, a miter joint is stronger than a simple butt joint.

Miter joints are widely used in the carpentry and cabinetmaking industry. The joint is popular because it's pleasing to look at and hides the end grain of each board.

These joints are used a great deal for building doors and drawers, and for the most part they are relatively simple to make. Two boards are joined at an angle. In almost all cases, the angle of each board is one-half the joint angle.

GROOVE, DADO AND RABBET JOINTS

Groove, dado and rabbet joints are all related and are made the same way. The position of the cut on a board determines its name. A groove is with the grain, a dado is cut across the grain and a rabbet is cut on the edge of a board.

Joints such as these, where a channel is cut into the wood, are easily made with a router or table saw. They are the most common joints used in the cabinetmaking industry. They are mechanically strong, easily made, and can be used in many situations — which is why they are so popular.

TONGUE-AND-GROOVE JOINTS

The tongue-and-groove (or tenon-and-groove) joint is quite often the joint of choice for many door styles. A raised-panel door has a groove cut in the rails and stiles and a tongue on the stile ends.

The closed groove or "track" formed by joining stiles and rails allows a panel to float in the frame. It's not necessary to mechanically bond the panel because it's supported on all sides.

MORTISE-AND-TENON JOINTS

This is one of the favorite woodworking joints. It's been used for centuries to join wood and continues to be commonly used by all woodworkers. The mortise or "hole" part of the joint can be cut on a drill press or with a dedicated mortise press. Holes can be left rounded at the corners or chiseled square. It's your preference — each method is strong.

Tenons can be formed by hand but are quickly and accurately made with a table saw. They can be cut with a tenoning attachment on the saw or with a dado blade. It's not important how this joint is made as long as the fit is perfect. It's one of the strongest woodworking joints that you can use.

FINGER (BOX) JOINTS

Finger joints are simple, decorative and mechanically strong because of the large glue surface created by the fingers. They can be cut by hand, on a router table, or by building a table saw jig.

In chapter nine I'll show you how to build an accurate finger-joint jig for a table saw. You'll use this joint for many applications, such as drawer-box construction; I use finger joints when building tool and blanket chests. It's also the perfect joint for large-cabinet work, so it's one worth mastering.

HAND CUT DOVETAIL JOINTS

The dovetail joint, with all its variations, is the most challenging joint to make but one of the strongest and finest furniture joints. It, like the box joint, has been a standard for centuries.

The process involves laying out the pin depth with a marking gauge on the outside face of the board. The pins are typically set at a 10° angle and are divided equally across the board end. The pins are cut with a dovetail saw and the completed profile is used to mark out the tails on the board to be joined. This hand-cut joint will be shown in step-by-step detail in chapter nine.

MACHINE-MADE DOVETAIL JOINTS

There are many dovetail jigs on the market today. A good, high-quality jig is relatively expensive but it will last you a lifetime. If you use dovetail joinery often, a good jig is well worth the money.

Research the different systems on the market. Look at how the metal is machined and what accessories are available. A poor jig will only make a poor joint. A high-quality jig will have a well-written manual and it's worth reading thoroughly. Follow the manufacturer's instructions and practice making the joint.

Use a carbide dovetail bit in your router and make certain it's sharp. The quality of the dovetail joint depends largely on clean, accurately cut pins and tails.

LAP JOINTS

Lap joints are modified rabbet or dado joints. The depth of cut on each piece is equal to half the board's thickness, so the two boards cross, or intersect, with the joint thickness equal to one board's thickness.

This joint is often used when two boards cross each other at a right angle. Frames or table support bases often are made with this joint. The cut is a dado when in the center of the two boards, and a rabbet when the joint is end to end. It's also common to see one board with a rabbet and one with a dado when the intersection forms a *T*.

COPE-AND-STICK JOINTS

Cope-and-stick joinery, sometimes called rail-and-stile, is widely used for door construction. The joint is made using router bit sets or shaper cutters. The two bit sets are the ones commonly used, with one to create a cope cut on the ends of each rail, and the other for the mirror image groove on the rail and stile edges.

A cope-and-stick joint is nothing more than a glorified mortise-and-tenon joint. Because these bits cut a fancy pattern, a great deal more surface area is formed which means stronger glue joints. There are quite a few profile patterns available to make a cabinet door frame that's classic or plain.

DOWELS AND BISCUITS

Dowels have long been used as a means to strengthen many types of joints. Biscuits, which are relatively new to woodworkers, are quickly becoming the preferred method of joint reinforcement.

You'll often hear the term biscuit joinery even though the proper name is plate joinery. However, the term biscuit has caught on, and only the manufacturers refer to the tool as a plate joiner.

Whatever the process is called, I believe it is one of the best woodworking inventions. Installing biscuits is much easier than aligning holes for dowels. In fact, once the biscuit joiner is adjusted, alignment is automatic.

Plate joinery involves cutting semicircular slots in both boards to be joined. Glue is applied to the edges of each board and in the slots. An oval-shaped beechwood biscuit is put in the slots on one board, then the boards are clamped.

Biscuits increase the gluing surface, and that's beneficial in achieving a stronger joint. But, more importantly, the beechwood ovals swell by absorbing the moisture in the glue and increase the joint's strength even further.

POCKET-HOLE JOINTS

Pocket-hole joinery is a relatively new method and, like biscuit joinery, will most likely take some time to be widely accepted. However, the practice of boring holes at an angle and using wood dowels to secure the joint is an old and accepted method. The system has been refined with modern hardware that takes the place of wood dowels. The screws offer a distinct advantage over dowels because they draw the parts together and do not require clamping.

EDGE JOINING FOR PANEL GLUE-UPS

Edge joinery is used to make solid-wood panels using a number of narrow boards. Biscuits may be used, but simple edge-to-edge contact with glue is the preferred method for door center panels.

Panels are prepared by dressing the edges on a jointer; a well-tuned table saw also may be used. I will outline the steps for successful edge joinery using your table saw later in this book so you don't have to spend money for a jointer. Straight, clean edges that contact each other without force, a coating of glue, and a few clamps will produce perfect solid panels for doors.

Ripping and crosscutting large panels may be quite a task at times, although the rip cut is normally a simple process with a good table saw fence. The crosscut, however, is difficult because panel ends aren't always in line after the glue-up. I suggest you build the crosscutting jig that's described in the Shop Talk on the next page to make that task a lot easier and safer.

SHOP TALK *Building a Panel Cross Cutting Jig*

Cut a piece of ³⁄₄"-thick sheet material that's approximately 24" wide by 36" long. You'll also need a strip of hardwood that fits snugly, without binding, in one of the miter slots on your table saw. The hardwood strip should be about 30" long so a few inches of the material will extend past the front and rear edges of the sheet. Most miter slots are ³⁄₄" wide and about ¹⁄₄" to ³⁄₈" deep. Attach the hardwood strip to the bottom face of the panel, parallel to one 24"-long edge. Draw a line parallel to the panel's edge to guide the strip placement, being sure to mark it so there's 1" of panel extending past the blade.

Place the panel, with the hardwood strip attached, in the miter slot and cut the panel overhang. This cut will align the panel travel parallel to the saw blade.

Use a carpenter's framing square to align a hardwood guide at 90° to the panel's cut edge. Secure the guide with screws.

Door and Drawer Hardware

The hardware used to mount doors and drawers demands that both fit properly and are correctly sized. The methods used to calculate the correct size for both drawers and doors will be discussed in this chapter.

There are differences between frameless and face-frame style cabinets that must be taken into consideration when doors and drawer boxes are installed. Two common door-hinge mounting styles are overlay and inset. The overlay door is attached to the cabinet or carcass box with hinges and partially covers the front edges of the cabinet. The inset door is set into the cabinet opening, flush with the outside face. There are of course variables on the two, including half-overlay and pocket-mounting styles. However, the two generally accepted terms for door-fitting styles are the overlay and inset door.

Drawer boxes that are mounted on mechanical slides also demand that you accurately size each box to its opening. In general, bottom-mount or full-extension side-and-bottom mounted glide sets require a $1/2$" space on each side of the drawer box for correct fitting. However, manufacturers have different specifications, so you should verify the space requirements before building the drawer box.

Many references in this book involve the hidden or concealed hinge. The popularity of the hidden hinge has grown so much that it's now the standard hinge for cabinetry. Traditional butt and overlay hinges are reasonably straightforward to install, so detailed explanations aren't necessary; but installing hidden hinges requires an understanding of their technical specifications and other issues. Those hinges, and modern drawer-glide hardware, will be the focus of this book with respect to mounting drawer boxes and doors.

FACE-FRAME VS. FRAMELESS CABINETS

You should be aware of the cabinet style before building cabinet doors and drawers. Are they *face-frame* or *frameless* cabinets? The two main styles of cabinets have many variations but can be generally classified by either style. However, being aware of which type you are building will help determine the door and drawer hardware requirements.

A face-frame cabinet has a solid-wood frame attached to the front edges of the cabinet box. A frameless-style cabinet has the carcass panel front edges covered with a tape, which can be paper or wood veneer. In many cases, the edge tape is applied with an iron that activates the adhesive.

The frameless cabinet is the one at the left in the photograph. Notice the similar construction methods for the face-frame cabinet on the right. It's a frameless cabinet with a solid-wood front frame attached.

EUROPEAN HINGES

Door-mounting hardware from Europe has become a very popular alternative. The so-called "Euro hidden hinge" is now widely used as the standard kitchen-cabinet door hardware.

The hidden hinge usually requires a hole drilled in the door. That task may seem a bit challenging to some people, but it's a straightforward process. Working with the hidden hinge does require familiarity with some new terms and concepts. For example, these hinges are classified with terms such as full-overlay, half-overlay and inset. Overlay refers to the amount of the cabinet's side panel covered by the door.

The hinge on top is a 170° wide-opening model and the one below is a standard 100° hinge. The hinge plate beside the top hinge is a standard cabinet side-mounting plate; the plate

below it is used to mount hinges on face frames. The face-frame mounting plate is used when the cabinet frame's inside stile edges are not flush with the inside face of the cabinet-box side panels.

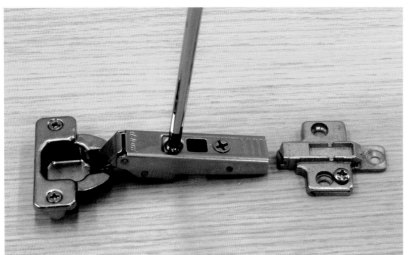

PARTS OF THE HIDDEN HINGE

The hidden hinge comes in two parts. The hinge boss, or body, which is mounted on the door in a 35mm-diameter hole. The mounting plate is attached to the cabinet side. The body is attached to the mounting plate with a screw or a clip pin. The clip-on method is popular because you can remove the door from the mounting plate without disturbing any adjustments.

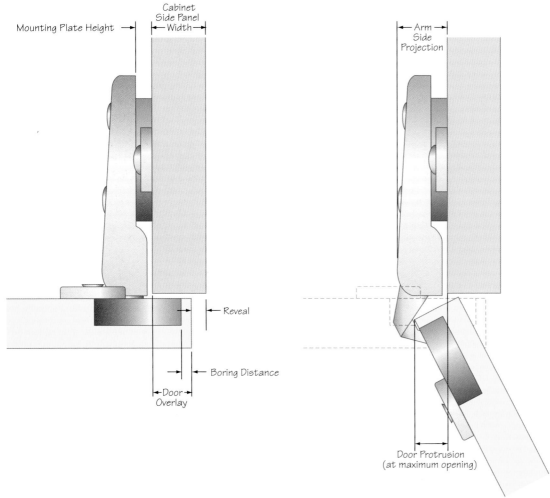

Mounting Plate Height

Cabinet Side Panel Width

Arm Side Projection

Reveal

Boring Distance

Door Overlay

Door Protrusion (at maximum opening)

HINGE OPENING

Hidden hinges are also classified in terms of degrees of opening. For standard door applications, the 100° to 120° opening hinge is common. You can also purchase hinges that will allow the door to open from 90° to 170°. The term simply refers to the number of degrees of swing allowed as the door opens from its closed position.

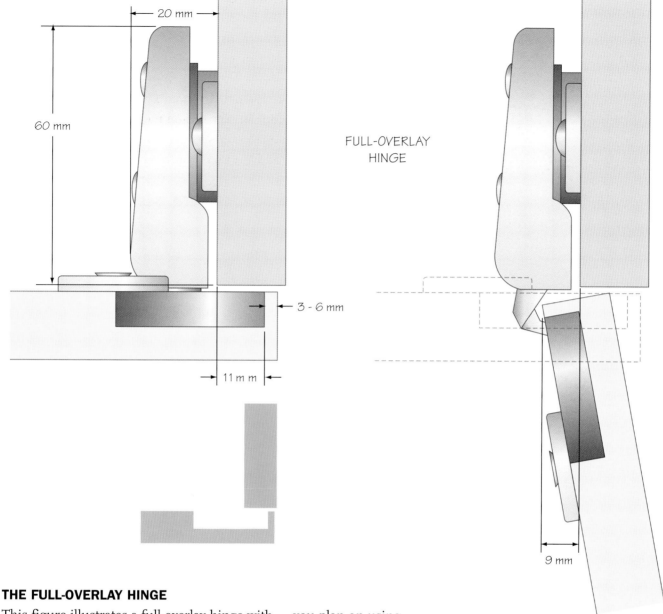

20 mm

60 mm

FULL-OVERLAY
HINGE

3 - 6 mm

11 m m

9 mm

THE FULL-OVERLAY HINGE

This figure illustrates a full-overlay hinge with the dimensions in millimeters. The door, when closed, almost covers the cabinet edge. That overlay distance is largely based on frameless European-style cabinetry that uses 16mm ($^5/_8$")-thick melamine-coated particleboard for kitchen-cabinet building.

Two 35mm-diameter holes are drilled in the door to accept the hinges. The holes are set back about $^1/_8$" from the door's edge. Most manufacturers of door hinges — including the type I use, made by Blum — require this setup. However, check the specifications supplied by the manufacturer of the hinges

you plan on using.

The depth of the hinge hole is dependent on the hinge. While there are slight variances, most hinges will fit in a hole that's $^1/_2$" deep. Again, check the specifications with the hinge you plan on using.

The ideal bit for drilling a hinge hole is flat-bottomed, often called a Forstner bit or a hinge-boring bit. I suggest you use carbide-tipped bits because binding adhesives used to manufacture particleboard and plywood sheet goods are hard, as are most of the woods used in door construction. High-speed steel bits will burn very quickly when drilling these boards.

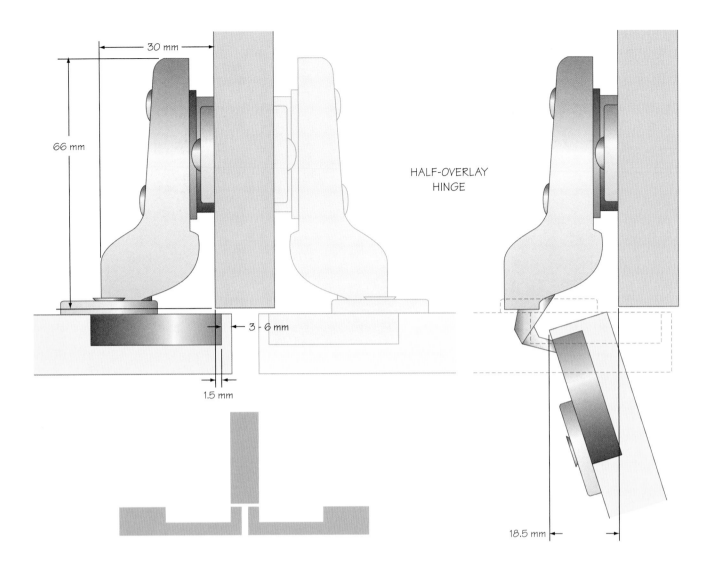

30 mm

66 mm

HALF-OVERLAY
HINGE

3 - 6 mm

1.5 mm

18.5 mm

THE HALF-OVERLAY HINGE

The half-overlay hinge is identical to the full-overlay model with one slight difference; it mounts on the door in the same way but the cabinet side-edge overlap is only about $^5/_{16}$", or one-half the full overlay.

Manufacturers call this a half-overlay hinge but you might see it referred to as a twin or dual-applica-tion hinge. This hinge is used when two doors meet on one side or dividing edge. That application may arise when you have a series of doors, side by side in a run, and the center doors meet on one divider panel. It's a limited-use hinge, but there are times when the smaller overlay is needed.

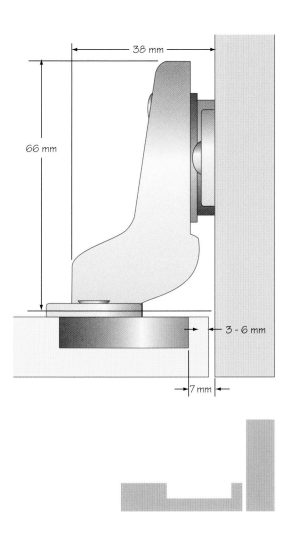

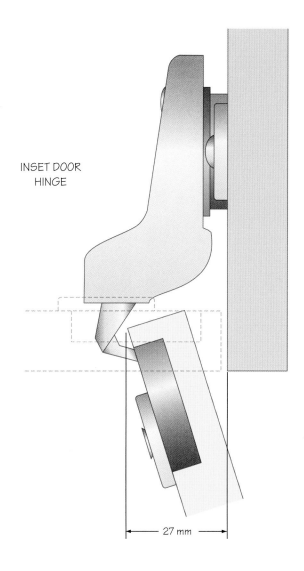

INSET DOOR
HINGE

THE INSET HINGE

The inset hinge is perfect for flush-mounted doors. The mechanical ability of this hinge in maintaining its position is an important feature. Unlike some of the earlier inset hinges and traditional North American styles, it's adjustable.

Building inset doors for any woodworking project is challenging. The cabinet opening must be square and the door has to be built with very close tolerances. Often, the clearance between the door and cabinet opening is $1/16$" or less. A high-quality hinge is necessary for this application.

Study the specifications on the hinge you plan to use before building your inset doors. There are slight mounting variances, depending on the manufacturer; you should be aware of these before the doors are built.

SHOP TALK *Installing the Hidden Hinge*

*There are door-mounting jigs avail-
able at all woodworking stores. If you
plan to use the hidden hinge for
many of your projects, these jigs are
very worthwhile. If you're using the
hidden hinge only occasionally,
here's a quick and easy installation
method that does not require a jig.*

*This method works with all hinge-
mounting applications. It's based on
using a 95° to 120° standard-opening
hinge. If you plan on installing a non-
standard hinge, such as the 170°
model, install the door with a standard-hinge body mounted in the door,
then replace it with a 170° body
after the door has been hung.*

First, drill the 35mm holes in the door for the hinge, ⅛" from the
door edge. The holes are typically 3" to 4" from each end; it's
not an important issue, so pick a distance where the hinge won't
interfere with anything in the cabinet.

Secure the hinge body in the hole making certain it's at 90° to
the door edge. Use ⅝"-long screws to anchor the hinge.

22

3 Attach the mounting plate to the hinge body.

4 Place the door on the cabinet in its 90° open position. A $\frac{1}{8}$"-thick spacer, between the door edge and the cabinet side edge, sets the correct door gap. Insert screws through the mounting plate to secure it to the cabinet side.

5

Remove the door by releasing the hinge bodies from the mounting plates. Insert the remaining screws in the mounting plates. This door-installation method will align the door in its proper position. All that may be needed are minor adjustments for a perfectly installed door on hidden hinges. If this is an application where you want to use a 170° wide-opening hinge, replace the standard-hinge body and install the door on the same mounting plates. The wider-opening hinge will also be correctly positioned.

FRAMELESS CABINET DOOR SIZES

If you plan to use the standard full-overlay hidden hinge, there's an easy rule of thumb to determine door size on frameless cabinets. The door height for upper cabinets is sized to cover both top and bottom board edges — the door equals the cabinet-box height.

Base-cabinet door heights, particularly with respect to kitchen cabinetry, are 1" less than the cabinet height. Countertop overhang can be up to $\frac{3}{4}$" below the cabinet's top board, so clearance is required. If the cabinet box is 31" high, not including the base frame, the door covers the bottom board edge and, at 30" high, leaves a 1" space at the top of the cabinet.

Door width is the critical issue. It's determined by first measuring the inside opening of the cabinet. Next, add 1" to that dimension to find the door width. For example, a utility cabinet that has a 21" inside opening measurement will need one 22"-wide door or two 11"-wide doors. It's that simple! You will have to adjust the hinges slightly to get the correct gap between doors. But as you'll discover, this simple rule works in almost all cases.

FACE-FRAME CABINET DOOR SIZES

Face-frame cabinet boxes are built much like a frameless box. However, the box (carcass) has an applied hardwood frame on the front face. The carcass can be made of sheet materials such as plywood or particleboards. In old cabinets you might see solid-wood panels that have been glued together.

In some instances, the face frame's inside dimension is less than the inside carcass dimension. The cabinet's side board is set back from the inside edge of the face-frame vertical members (stiles). If that's the type of face-frame cabinet you're building or you encounter one that needs new doors, you can use traditional North American-style hinges or hidden hinges with a face-frame mounting plate. Either hinge will work fine.

In the last few years, cabinetmakers — particularly in the kitchen cabinetmaking industry — have installed face frames so the inside edge of the face-frame stiles are flush with the inside face of the cabinet.

The measurement process for doors on face-frame cabinets is the same as frameless when using hidden hinges. Measure the distance between the inside stile edges of the face frame and add 1" to that dimension. That will determine cabinet door width.

The door height on face-frame cabinet uppers and bases is 1" to $1\frac{1}{4}$" less than the face-frame height. The door covers the bottom face-frame rail and leaves room at the top of the frame. Base units need the top clearance for countertop overhang and upper cabinets use the top free space for applied moldings.

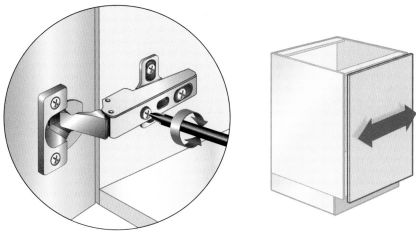

HORIZONTAL ADJUSTMENT

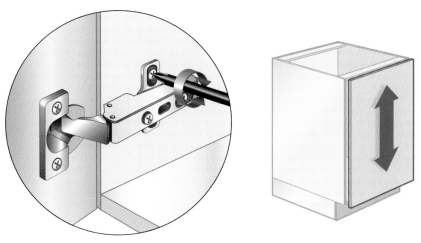

VERTICAL ADJUSTMENT

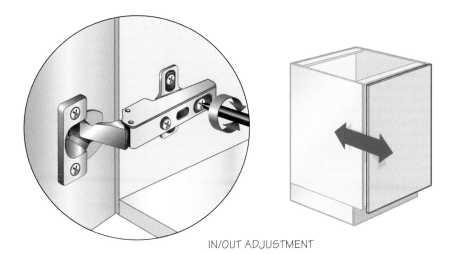

IN/OUT ADJUSTMENT

ADJUSTING HIDDEN HINGES

Hidden hinges can be adjusted to move the cabinet door in three directions. The adjustment screw functions are fairly straightforward. With minor style differences, most hinges can be adjusted as shown in the illustration.

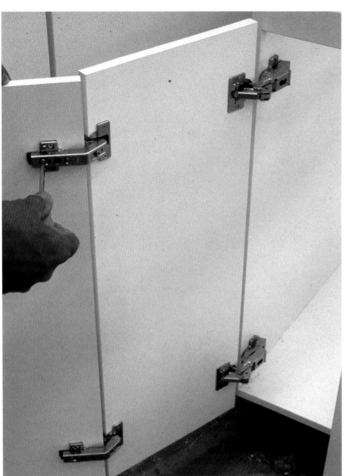

WIDE-OPENING AND BIFOLD HINGES

There are many special application hinges, such as the 170° wide-opening hinge and the bifold hinge, which normally come with detailed installation instructions or technical specification sheets that are available from the hardware supplier.

POCKET DOOR HINGES

The pocket-door hinge system is another of the specialized hinges that will be fully described in this book. Pocket door hinge systems are often used when building television armoires. There are door-sizing and installation issues to deal with, but this is a fairly simple hardware system for hidden doors.

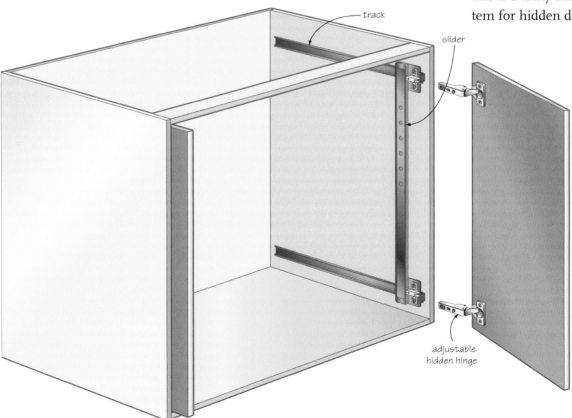

track

slider

adjustable hidden hinge

DRAWER-BOX CONSTRUCTION

There are dozens of methods used to build drawer boxes; I'll go through the step-by-step process for many of them in this book. The joinery used can be as simple as a butt joint or as intricate as a drawer lock or dovetail joint. There are also dozens of material choices for drawer-box construction, including melamine particleboard, Baltic birch plywood and solid wood.

Drawers used to be tracked on wood runners, so the material choice — as well as the construction style — was limited. However, the newer drawer-tracking hardware allows us to use more types of materials and different construction techniques.

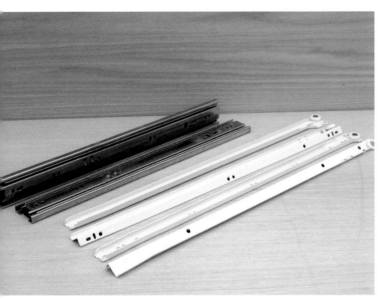

DRAWER HARDWARE

Modern drawer hardware has opened a great many possibilities for drawer-box design and construction. The white glides shown in the photograph are typical of the bottom-mount sets that are available on the market. They are often referred to as three-quarter drawer slides because they allow the drawer to be pulled out three-quarters of the set length. For example, a standard 22"-long drawer-glide set will let the drawer box travel about $16\frac{1}{2}$". The silver set is a full-extension (FX) glide that allows full outward travel of the drawer box. The mechanics incorporated into the FX set are more involved, which is why these slides are approximately three times the cost of standard three-quarter glides.

These mechanical slides have improved drawer-box operation when compared to the old-style wood runners, and they are much more reliable. However, they do demand that you pay a great deal of attention to drawer-box sizing.

DRAWER BOX SIZE CALCULATION

The two cabinet styles, face-frame and frameless, each have formulas for calculating the correct drawer-box size. Most hardware requires a $\frac{1}{2}$" space on both sides of the box to properly install the hardware. The Shop Talk sections in chapter nine will outline the steps so you can build boxes and drawer faces that fit — no matter which style of cabinet you build.

Building Slab Doors

Slab or flat panel doors are the simplest form of cabinet doors. In most cases, they are made using sheet materials such as veneer plywood or particleboard (PB), melamine PB, medium-density fiberboard (MDF), or solid-wood glued-up panels.

These flat panels can be edge-taped with a matching material, solid-wood edged, or formed when the edges are solid material. Because these doors are flat, moldings can be applied to create visual interest or a pattern can be routed into the face. In many cases, slab doors made with materials like MDF sheet stock can be painted.

They are relatively inexpensive because a 4' × 8' sheet will yield quite a few doors. However, because they are flat they can look plain but we can add some interesting details with mouldings and decorative scroll pieces. Designs can be cut into the face of solid-wood panels and

MDF sheet stock using the pattern-routing jig described at the end of this chapter.

There are dozens of ways to make panel doors and just as many ways to add detailing. I'll show you a few in this chapter with some of the sheet stock material that's available.

Doors are the most expensive part of any cabinet project, so using sheet material is one way to keep the cost at a reasonable level. And with a little imagination — using paint, designs, mouldings and routing techniques — slab doors can add a great deal to the overall look of your cabinet project.

Melamine PB Doors

Melamine PB doors are typically flat doors cut from a sheet of 4' × 8', $^5/_8$"- or $^3/_4$"-thick melamine particleboard. They are low-cost doors because a sheet will yield quite a few doors at about $1 per square foot. The edges are finished with iron-on tape that is available in many colors to match the sheet stock. White melamine PB is the most common sheet material on the market.

These doors have many uses, such as for workshop and laundry room cabinets or for basic storage cabinetry in your home. The colored sheets can be used to create work and storage cabinets for children's rooms or in a basement playroom.

Cut the melamine sheet material to the door size required and apply tape to all exposed edges. The most common edge tape available has an adhesive back, which is activated with an iron. Be sure to roll the tape when the glue is hot to achieve full edge contact.

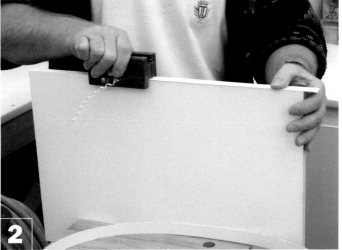

Trim the edge tape to the board thickness with a two-sided edge trimmer, sharp chisel or knife.

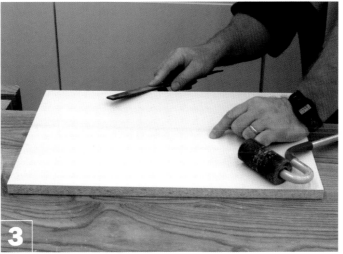

Dress the edges with a laminate file, removing any portion of the tape that extends past the board's face. A smooth surface between edge tape and door face will help prevent damage to the tape.

Veneer-Slab Doors

Veneer-slab doors can be made using veneer-covered particleboard or plywood sheet material. The construction steps used to build this type of flat panel door are much the same as for melamine PB doors. Wood-veneer tape, which matches the face veneer, is used to dress the panel edges. However, there are special cutting techniques that must be used when edge-dressing the tape.

Apply the wood-veneer edge tape using an iron to activate the adhesive. Roll the tape as it's heated to ensure a good bond between the tape and board edges.

Wood-veneer edge tape is real wood as the name suggests. It has a wood species — oak, for example — and a grain structure that tends to split along the grain line when trimmed with a knife. Using a router and flush-trim router bit with a guide bearing helps to ensure a clean cut without splitting the veneer.

Light passes with fine sandpaper can be used to smooth the tape edges. The edge between the tape and the board face, should be smooth to lessen the chance of tape damage.

Wood-Edged Doors

Solid wood can be used to dress the edges of veneer-slab doors. It's a tougher edge treatment that opens up a few options not available with edge-taped doors. The solid-wood edge can be machined with a router using a roundover or chamfer bit to add a little more detail to these flat doors.

SHOP SAFETY NOTE

Before you start ripping the thin strips of wood needed to dress the edges, refer to the instructions in chapter eight on making a thin-strip push stick that will keep your fingers far away from the blade.
I suggest that you use this push stick when cutting thin material on your table saw.

1 Cut the slab door to the required size less ½" on the width and length. Rip ¼"-thick solid-wood strips on the table saw and attach them to the door slab. Use glue and small brad nails to secure the wood strips. The first two strips are attached on opposite edges, aligning one end of each strip flush with the board end. Notice that I've cut the wood strips longer than the door length.

2 Set the table-saw fence to the panel length and trim the long ends of the wood strips. The strips will be perfectly flush with the panel ends.

31

SAFETY NOTE

As mentioned in the front pages of this book, I have removed the guards on my power tools to show the details of each operation. The guards are always in place when the tools are under power. Notice that blades, drills and other cutting tools are stopped for the photograph. I have replaced the guards during the actual cutting and machining operations and strongly suggest that you use them and follow all safety precautions when operating power tools.

Follow the same procedures, as detailed in step two, for the remaining two strips. Install and trim to length on the table saw. Use colored wood filler that matches the final door finish to fill the nail holes. Sand the wood edges smooth.

The solid-wood edges can be machined with a router. A roundover bit (shown in the photograph) or a chamfer bit are two common edge treatments for these doors, but there are many styles of bits that may be used.

Solid Wood Slab Doors

Solid-wood doors can be a nice addition to any cabinet project. Because they are solid, these slab doors can be machined using many more techniques than is possible with melamine or veneer-covered slab doors.

The process used to make solid-wood doors starts with the glue-up process of narrow boards to form a large panel. The edges of the narrow boards are machined straight and flat so all boards fit tight to each other. Usually a jointer is used to dress the boards, but a table saw may be used by following a few simple steps.

Edge-dressing narrow boards for solid-wood glued-up panels can be done on a well-tuned table saw. First, be sure the fence will tightly lock into place and is running parallel to the saw blade. The blade rotation must be smooth, without end play, to get the straight cuts on each board that are needed for successful glue ups. Rip one edge of the board; then turn it around, keeping the same face up, and rip the other edge. Both edges should be parallel to each other and at 90° to the board's face.

Remove small portions of the board's edge during each cut. Make sure that the edges are parallel with the board's face.

Test the boards by pushing them together on a flat surface. They should butt tightly to each other without a great deal of pressure. If necessary, repeat the edge-ripping steps until the boards fit together properly.

Apply glue to all the edges that are to be joined. Use clamps, alternating on the top and bottom, to bring the boards together. Don't apply too much clamp pressure or you will squeeze out all the glue and your joints will fail.

Use a panel crosscutting jig (see Shop Talk, chapter one) to square the ends and trim the door to its proper length. Then, rip the width to the correct size.

The edges can be machined with any bit profile, including a roundover in a router, as shown. You can also use profile bits such as a cove, ogee or chamfer to add visual interest to the door.

More Wood-Slab Door Options

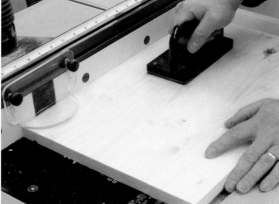

Woodworkers who have a router table can use it to create dozens of single and multiple profiles on slab doors. The fence systems used with routers in a table will let you accurately align the door to a cutting bit for one or a number of identical passes.

There's an unlimited amount of machining and detail that can be added to flat slab doors. Here are a couple of ideas using a router table, and another if you have some artistic talent.

Chamfer, bullnose, V-groove and double-profile bits can be used in the router table to create interesting designs in wood slab doors. I used a bullnose bit, 1" in from the door edges, to create this cross pattern.

Those of you who paint can add your special touch to slab doors. These artistic, one-of-a-kind doors, add a unique touch to any cabinet project.

Applied-Moulding Slab Doors

Veneer-core slab doors with taped or wood edges can be "dressed" up by adding mouldings. These are available at lumber yards and woodworking stores. There are dozens of patterns and styles that can be attached to the door

When applying mouldings to slab doors, the first step is to accurately mark the moulding position on your doors. This is important for achieveing a balanced-looking door.

Wood moulding can be attached to veneer doors using a little glue and small brad nails. Some mouldings are delicate, so they must be handled carefully.

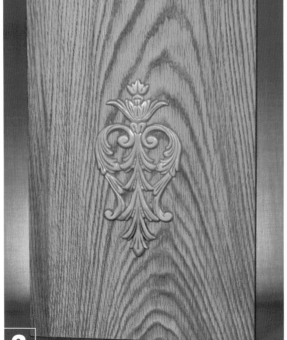

You can also buy intricate scroll-work patterns in wood that can be attached to slab doors. The same process applies; a little glue and a couple of brad nails are all that's needed. Or, if you have a scroll saw, you can make your own unique door-trim mouldings.

SHOP TALK *Making a Laminate Cutting Jig*

Cutting high-pressure laminate material makes me nervous. These thin, hard laminate sheets break easily and can have sharp edges that easily cut and bruise. I've always had a healthy respect for laminates when cutting them. This cutting jig increases the safety factor when handling high-pressure laminates (HPL) by trapping the material so it can't slide and jam under the saw fence.

Cut a piece of straight sheet stock that's about 30" long. Attach a 30" length of hardboard that's 2" wide to the underside of the board with screws. Round off the leading and trailing edge of a wood block that's about 6" long. It should be attached to the board face $1/16$" above the hardboard and in the middle of the straight stock.

Secure the new jig fence to the existing table saw fence so the wood block is directly across from the saw blade. The HPL material passes between the wood block and lower hardboard so that it's trapped. The hardboard is held tight to the underside of this auxiliary fence and will not slip under the fence to cause a potentially serious laminate jam. If your saw is equipped with an overarm blade guard, lower it to ride on the laminate as it travels through the blade. This will eliminate HPL "chatter" as it passes through the blade and increase the material control. This simple jig can be used on any table saw and building one is well worth your time and effort. Stopping the thin laminates from sliding under the fence during cutting will prevent a common accident from happening when cutting laminates.

Making P-Lam Doors

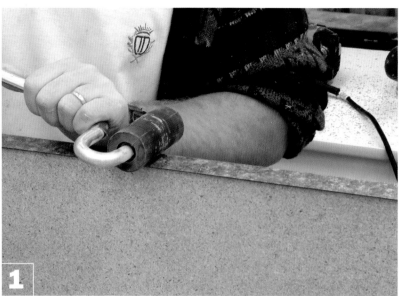

Cut the door blank using ¾"-thick particleboard (PB) sheet material. Next, using the laminate cutting jig, rip 1"-wide strips of HPL that are long enough to cover the four door blank edges. Cut these strips 1" longer than needed to allow for position errors. Apply a coat of contact cement to all the door blank edges and the back of each strip. Follow the directions on the contact cement container with regard to adhesive set-up time and application methods. Once the cement is cured, attach the strips one at a time and use a pressure roller to be sure the HPL is firmly bonded to the door blank.

P-Lam is a term often used to describe doors made with a covering of high-pressure laminate (HPL) material. These doors are popular in some areas and are often used for kitchen refacing projects. HPL is durable and is available in a wide range of colors and patterns. It's often the door of choice for commercial cabinet projects in stores and offices because the material is durable.

Trim each strip so it's flush with the door-blank edges and ends using a flush-trim bit with guide bearing in a router. Follow the same steps until all four edges of the blank are covered and trimmed.

Cut two pieces of HPL material 1" wider and longer than the door-blank face. Apply a coat of contact cement to the door face and laminate back. Lay thin strips of wood on the door and position the laminate, making sure there is overhang on all edges. The wood strips will not stick to either piece because they are not coated with contact cement. Once the HPL is correctly aligned, pull the center stick out and press down to bind the two surfaces. Repeat the steps, working out from the center of the door.

Use a laminate pressure roller to complete the bond. Roll from the center outwards to drive any air bubbles out from between the HPL and the door blank.

Once again, use a flush-trim router bit to trim both faces even with the side edges.

To complete the P-Lam door, dress the laminate edges with a fine-tooth file. These special files are designed for HPL material. The HPL door is now ready to be installed.

Medium Density Fiberboard (MDF) Doors

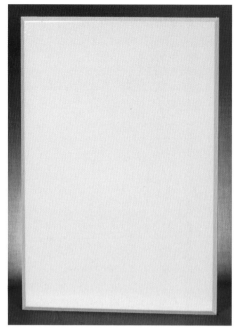

MDF doors are inexpensive because a 4' × 8' sheet of $^3/_4$"-thick material will provide a lot of doors. MDF doors often have moldings attached or are edge-routed, and they are usually painted.

Many different router bits can be used to decorate MDF edges. A chamfer bit (shown here) creates one style, but you can use cove, roundover or design cutters with profiles like a Roman ogee. MDF sheet material can be machined with standard woodworking tools. It's also possible to cut center patterns in MDF or solid-wood panels using the pattern-routing jig described in the following Shop Talk session.

SHOP TALK *Building a Pattern-Routing Jig*

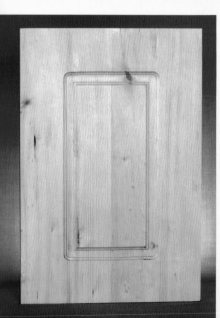

Center-pattern cutting on door blanks is often done on computer numerically controlled (CNC) machines. These are expensive woodcutting tools, but you can build a manual pattern jig for your door blanks.

This jig will cut a pattern on doors from 10" to 20" wide and 10" to 30" *high, which should take care of just about any project door you'll need. The plunge router is fitted with a cutter that has a fancy profile, which is lowered into the door face. These router bits are readily available at all woodworking stores.*

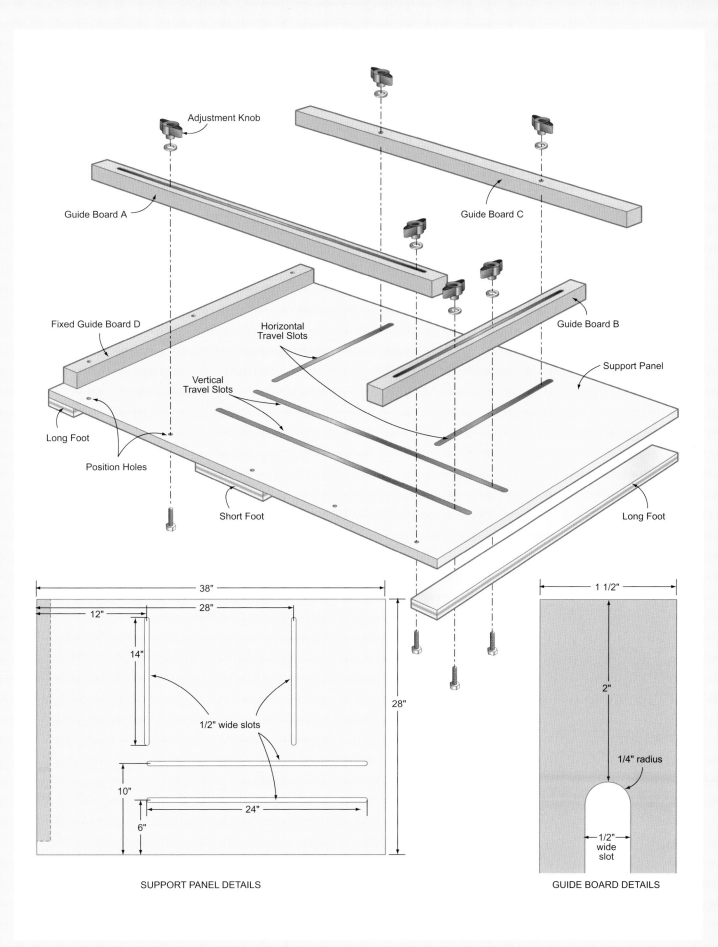

Adjustment Knob

Guide Board A

Guide Board C

Fixed Guide Board D

Horizontal
Travel Slots

Guide Board B

Support Panel

Vertical
Travel Slots

Long Foot

Position Holes

Short Foot

Long Foot

SUPPORT PANEL DETAILS

38"

28"

12"

14"

28"

1/2" wide slots

10"

24"

6"

GUIDE BOARD DETAILS

1 1/2"

2"

1/4" radius

1/2"
wide
slot

41

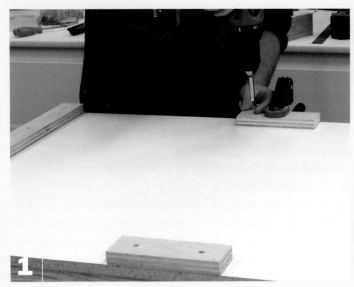

1 Cut a base panel for the jig using ⅝" PB or any other sheet material of the same thickness that's 28" wide by 38" long. At either end, attach a "foot" that is 2" wide by 28" long and ¾" thick using 1¼" screws. Attach two additional feet that are 2" wide by 6" long on the side edges, as shown. All the support feet are aligned flush with the support panel edges. These feet will raise the support panel so the bolt heads attached to the adjustable knobs will be able to move freely.

2 Turn the support panel over and draw cut guide lines, beginning 2" in from the panel edges, in the positions shown on the drawing.

3 Use a ½" diameter straight-cutting bit in your router to cut slots through the board. Place a straightedge on the panel to guide your router along the previously drawn lines.

4 You'll need to cut four guide boards that are 1½" square. Guides A and C are 36" long and guides B and D are 24" long. Guides A and B require ½"-wide through-slots centered along the length of each board. The slot cuts start and end 2" from each end on both boards. Use a ½" diameter straight bit to cut the slots. Make a number of small passes on each guide board, plunging the boards onto the bit and lifting them off the bit 2" from the ends. You need to remove a lot of material, which will place a great deal of stress on the router bit, so remove only a little bit of material on each pass.

Attach the top-fixed guide D to the support panel with three 2"-long screws. It should be aligned flush with the outside top edge of the panel and flush with the right panel side, as shown, and should be 26½" long.

Guide A will be adjustable vertically along the left edge of the panel. Drill ⅜"-diameter holes about 6" apart along the panel edge so guide A will be aligned with the left edge of the panel. Use 3"-long ⁵⁄₁₆" bolts, two large fender washers, a lock washer and a ⁵⁄₁₆" threaded knob to secure the guide. The bolts can be moved to different holes depending on the amount of vertical travel that's required for the size of door you are routing.

7

Guide C is attached to the panel with the same size bolts and knobs in holes drilled through the guide, which are aligned to the horizontal travel slots.

8

Install guide B using the same bolts, washers and knobs. It will be able to travel vertically in the panel slots and horizontally in the guide slot.

A door blank can now be placed in the pattern guide. It's positioned tightly against the fixed guides D and A. Guide A should be moved vertically so its bottom end is in line with the door blank end. Next, slide guide C in the slots so it's tight to the open side of the door blank. Now move guide B vertically to the bottom edge of the door, which will now be held securely by the four guide posts. Position the router, with the bit raised, against one of the guide posts. Turn on the router and plunge the bit into the door blank to begin the cut pattern. Hold the router base tight to the guide posts as you move it around the inner frame. Raise the bit, turn off the router, and remove it from the frame.

9

ADDITIONAL BIT PROFILES

I used a bullnose bit for my first pattern. However, as previously mentioned, there are many styles of bits available at woodworking stores. Buy the bits that can be plunged into a panel and experiment with a few designs.

For this example, I'm using a pattern bit and cutting into a solid-wood door. However, this is only to show another bit profile. I'm hesitant to recommend cutting patterns in solid wood because there is a risk that the door will warp because of the deep cuts. MDF and other sheet goods that will be painted are the best materials to use for one-piece doors with a design.

MOULDING HEAD CUTTER DESIGNS

A moulding head cutter on a table saw is an excellent way to edge-profile solid doors. There are dozens of pattern cutters available that will allow you to cut some unique designs on your slab doors.

Frame and Flat Panel Doors

Frame and flat panel doors are built using five parts. Two vertical members of the door called stiles, two horizontal members called rails, and a center panel that's usually veneer core plywood. The term "flat panel" refers to the plywood veneer center panel. In later chapters I'll show you how to build the same style door using solid wood "raised" center panels.

The center panel of these doors isn't always $\frac{1}{4}$" thick plywood veneer. The two stiles and two rails are often joined in the same manner with sheet glass or decorative leaded glass center panels. I'll detail these and other panel options that are available in this chapter.

Corner joinery, or attaching the stiles to the rails, is the main concern with five piece doors. There are a number of methods using a table saw, router table, and mortising machine that can be used to form the joints. The steps are simple and straightforward but good woodworking practices must be used to produce solid frames.

This chapter will also deal with doors that have an arch or cathedral style cut on the top, bottom, or both rails. Making this style of door is a little more challenging but the procedures can be successfully mastered using simple geometry.

Table-Saw Tenon-and-Groove Doors

This style of door is made using a table saw only. The project door will be 12" wide by 18" high. The stiles and rails are solid 2¼"-wide solid wood, which are ¾" thick. The center panel is ¼"-thick veneer-covered plywood.

Cut the stiles and rails to the proper length. I normally use ¾"-thick by 2¼"-wide stock for my door frames. The rail tenons are ¾" long to match the grooves in the stiles. This combination of rail and stile width along with tenon length and groove depth makes it easy to calculate door-part dimensions. Refer to the Shop Tip and see how quickly you can calculate door-part sizes. Each rail and stile needs a ¼"-wide groove that's ¾" deep, centered on one long edge. Cut the groove with a standard blade in two passes. Reverse the feed direction on the second pass to center the groove. Or, you can use a stacked dado blade set to cut a ¼"-wide slot centered on the edge of each part.

The tenons on both ends of the two rails are ¼" thick by ¾" long. They should be centered on the rail ends to fit the stile grooves. Tenons can be cut using a standard table-saw blade or a stacked dado blade. Cut a sample tenon and test-fit the assembly before forming the tenons on the actual rails.

3

The center panel is ¼" thick veneer plywood to match the rails and stiles. I'm using solid-oak wood and veneer plywood, but any species of wood may be used. The center panel is 3" less in width and height as previously detailed in the Shop Tip. My 12"-wide by 18"-high door requires a panel that's 9" wide by 15" high. However, I usually cut the center panel ⅛" less in width and height to allow for wood movement. Cut the panel to size and test-fit the door parts.

4

Assemble the door with glue on the rail tenons only. The center panel isn't normally glued in place, but left to float. Clamp the door, then measure the diagonals. If both measurements are the same, the door is square. If there is a difference, lightly tap the long measurement diagonal to equalize the dimensions before the adhesive sets up.

SHOP TIP

The rail width equals the door width minus the stile widths. However, you also have to account for the tenon lengths on each end of the rail. A 12"-wide door with 2¼"-wide stiles requires a 7½"-wide rail, but you also need an additional 1½" for the tenons. The rough rail length before tenons are cut is therefore 9". With the ¾"-long tenons, ¾"-deep grooves and 2¼"-wide stiles, the rough rail length will always be 3" less than the door width. For example, using the same part dimensions, a 19"-wide door requires a 16" rail before tenons are cut — it's that easy when using the above combination of door-part dimensions. Center panel dimensions are easily calculated as well. The sample setup means the ¼" plywood panels will be 3" less than the overall door width and height. Therefore, the panel for a 12"-wide by 18"-high door will be 9" wide by 15" high.

Router Table Tenon-and-Groove Doors

These doors are made following the same procedures that I detailed for the table saw. However, my slot cutter can only cut a groove that's $1/2$" deep so the tenon dimensions will be reduced to $1/2$" in length. If you have a wing or slot cutter that cuts at $3/4$" deep, use that length of tenon. Cut the rails and stiles to length, then rout a $1/4$"-wide by $1/2$"-deep groove along one edge of each part. Be sure to center the grooves on the rails and stiles.

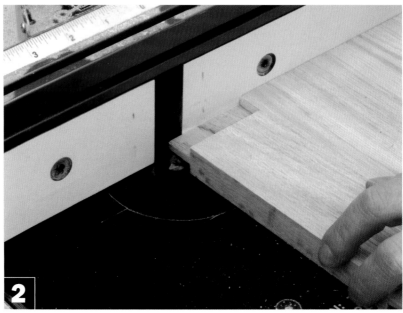

Replace the slot bit with a $1/2$" router bit to cut the rail tenons on each end. Once again, use a test piece of wood to center the tenon and verify its proper thickness. The tenons should fit snugly into the rail grooves without distorting the sides of those grooves. A loose fit will result in the joint failing, while a tight fit will put stress on the groove walls and may split the stile.

3

My slot cutter will only cut a $^3/_{16}$"-wide groove, but I want a $^1/_4$" groove. If you have a tool that won't cut the full width, set the bottom edge of the cutter $^1/_4$" about the router table surface. Make the first cutting pass, then flip the wood and make a final pass. The groove will be $^1/_4$" wide and centered when using $^3/_4$"-thick stock.

Cut the $^1/_4$"-thick center panel to the correct size and test-fit the door assembly. Once you are satisfied with the fit, apply glue to the tenons, install the center panel, and clamp until the adhesive sets up. Remember, the panel's width and height should be $^7/_8$" greater than the inside dimension of the door frame because the grooves are $^1/_2$" deep in my case. The panel should have a little space to allow for wood movement of the stiles and rails.

SHOP TALK *Decorative Door Options*

There are many edge options that you can use to add visual interest to your doors. Most are easily formed with router bits, including the cove, roundover and ogee. However, there are dozens more profiles, so experiment with a few until you find one that suits your taste.

There's one situation that can cause problems if the door-edge detail is cut too deep. Hinges, particularly European hidden hinges, rest in holes that are about $^1/_2$" deep and $^1/_8$" away

from the door's edge. Always test a profile cut on scrap lumber, then mount a sample hinge to determine if there will be proper clearance and sufficient material left for the hinge hole. Other traditional hinges, such as butt or piano hinges, require a full-thickness edge to be properly installed. The combination of door profile and hinge style may present a problem, so always test your setups before making the final cut.

49

Mitered Frame-and-Panel Door

Mitered corners on cabinet doors are often used to give the door a "furniture" look when compared to kitchen cabinet doors, which are usually butt joined. Mitered joints can be a little difficult to align and join, so biscuits or splines are commonly used at each corner.

Rail and stile width is a matter of personal taste, but I usually stay with the 2¼"-wide size for these doors. Biscuits are available in three sizes, No.20, No.10 and No.0, with No.20 being the largest. There is an FF-size biscuit which is smaller than the No.0 size and is the one most

often used for frame corner joinery. Some plate cutters are not equipped with a smaller blade to cut the slots for FF biscuits, so check the specifications of your tool.

The door I'm making is 12" wide by 18" high using ¾"-thick solid wood. There are three center panel options: ¼"-thick plywood veneer, solid raised panel, or glass. I'll detail the steps required to make a mitered door with a ¼"-thick veneer plywood panel and a ⅛"-thick glass center panel. The steps are slightly different because glass panels must be removable in case a replacement is needed.

Cut the rails and stiles 2¼" wide using ¾"-thick solid wood. The stiles are 18" long to the longest points of the 45° miters at both ends and the rails are 12" long for a 12"-wide by 18"-high door. Use a miter saw to prepare the four parts, making sure your saw is correctly aligned.

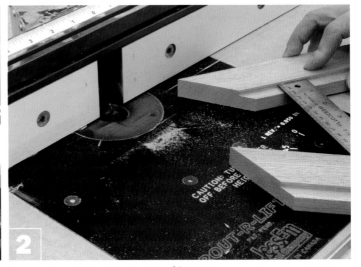

If your door will be fitted with a ¼"-thick veneer plywood center panel, cut grooves on the short edges of the stiles and rails. The grooves should be centered on the edges and should be ¾" deep. If you plan to use glass as a center panel, cut a ½"-wide by ¼"-deep rabbet on the short edge of all stiles and rails. The rabbets can be cut with a stacked dado blade on the table saw or a router bit in your router table.

Slots should be cut in the stile and rail miters using a biscuit cutter. Carefully align the cuts so they'll match up properly when the biscuits are installed. In some cases, the biscuits will extend into the miter or rabbet cuts, but they can be marked and trimmed before installing and gluing the joints. Be sure the slots are aligned and cut so they don't extend past the long points of each miter cut or they will be visible on the door edges.

Assemble the door frame using glue on the biscuits and clamp securely. Check the diagonal measurements to ensure the frame is square and adjust if necessary before the glue sets up.

Accurately measure the center panel size leaving ⅛" on both the width and height for wood movement. Install the glass panel and secure it with small brad nails or glass points. These points are available at all hardware stores and are commonly used to hold glass panels. This method may be used to create door frames for other types of decorative panels such as leaded glass or punched tin.

Mortise-and-Tenon Door Frames

Door frames can be built using mortise-and-tenon joinery. Tenons are cut on the ends of each rail and a mortise is formed in the stiles. This is a traditional joinery option that is still widely used.

The tenons may be cut by hand, on the table saw or on a router table, and the mortises formed with a drill press and chisel. I will be using a dedicated mortiser to cut my tenons because that's the method I prefer. If you use mortise-and-tenon joinery a lot, a dedicated mortiser would be a good investment.

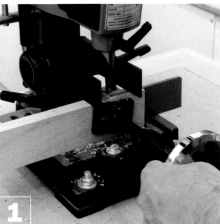

Cut the two stiles and rails to size to build a 12"-wide by 18"-high door. The stiles should be 18" high and the rails 9" wide when you're using $2\frac{1}{4}$" wide stiles and rails with $\frac{3}{4}$"-long tenons. The stiles need a $\frac{3}{4}$" deep mortise that's $1\frac{3}{4}$" long in the center at each end. Start all the mortises $\frac{1}{2}$" from each stile end. As mentioned, if you don't own a dedicated mortiser, drill a series of holes and clean out the waste with a sharp chisel to square the holes.

Form a $\frac{3}{4}$"-long by $\frac{1}{4}$"-thick tenon in the center of each rail end. The top outside $\frac{1}{2}$" of the tenons are notched so they will fit in the stile mortises that begin $\frac{1}{2}$" from each stile end. The tenons can be notched after they are cut to size with the same saw setup.

Brush glue on the tenons, then assemble the door if you plan on cutting rabbets on the back face for a glass panel. The door frame's back face needs a rabbet cut to hold the center panel. Glass, veneer plywood, or any type of decorative panel may be used. The rabbet is cut with a router bit called a slot cutter. It's equipped with a guide bearing that will follow the inside perimeter of the frame. You may need to make a number of passes with the slot cutter to achieve the desired rabbet depth. That depth will depend on the thickness of material used for the center panel. If you want a centered wood panel, use the same slot bit to cut the grooves. As stated before, my slot cutter is only $\frac{3}{16}$" thick, so I have to make two passes. Moreover, it only grooves $\frac{1}{2}$" deep, so my center panel for this 12"-wide by 18"-high door will be $8\frac{3}{8}$" wide by $14\frac{3}{8}$" high, which leaves a little space for wood movement. Once the cuts for the panel you want to install are completed, glue and clamp the frame.

SHOP TALK *Cathedral Doors*

Cutting curves, arcs and other radius patterns in rails is a little more difficult than cutting a straight-rail door. There are patterns for arched doors that can be purchased at woodworking stores. However, a little bit of simple geometry and an understanding of how the arc is varied based on door width will allow you to make your own patterns.

The arched door has a curve cut into the top rail and is referred to as an arched frame-and-panel door. I'll explain how the top rail can be cut to form a cathedral-style door later in this chapter. The important issue to remember is that kitchen doors vary in width. The challenge is to maintain a visually consistent appearance among all the doors in the room, no matter what width. To accomplish

this, all curves in each door must follow certain rules. I'm using $3\frac{1}{4}$"-wide upper curved rails for this example.

The straight stiles and bottom rail are $2\frac{1}{4}$" wide in my design. So, to maintain a consistent appearance between a door that's 12" wide and one that is 24" wide, I need a constant reference point on both doors. I can achieve a consistent look among all my doors by making sure my arc is $2\frac{1}{4}$" down from the top center of all the curved rails — no matter the door width. All my doors will have the same measurement above the arc and only the radius of the arc will change.

The drawing illustrates the differences between rails for a 12"-wide door and a 24"-wide door. Only the

rail width and arc radius change; all other values remain the same. The start and end of each arc is at the point where the rail meets the stiles. In addition, there should always be $2\frac{1}{4}$" of solid wood above, the center of each arc.

Starting and ending the arc at the same place on doors of different widths, as well as maintaining the $2\frac{1}{4}$" measurement above the arc, will make all the doors appear similar. Changing those fixed points as the width changes would dramatically change the door's appearance. You can verify these design principles by measuring different arched doors of different widths in any typical kitchen.

For detailed calculations on how to determine the radius of an arc for any door, refer to chapter six.

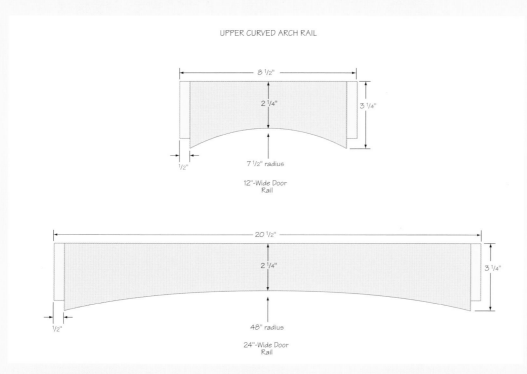

UPPER CURVED ARCH RAIL

8 1/2"
2 1/4"
3 1/4"
1/2"
7 1/2" radius
12"-Wide Door Rail

20 1/2"
2 1/4"
3 1/4"
1/2"
48" radius
24"-Wide Door Rail

Building Arched Frame-and-Panel Doors

This example door is 12" wide and 18" high. I'm using $\frac{3}{4}$"-thick stock for the stiles and rails with a $\frac{1}{4}$"-thick veneer plywood panel. All stock used for the doors is $\frac{3}{4}$" thick. Cut two stiles at $2\frac{1}{4}$" wide by 18" long and one upper rail at $3\frac{1}{4}$" high by $8\frac{1}{2}$" wide. The bottom rail is $2\frac{1}{4}$" high by $8\frac{1}{2}$" wide. Note that the width of the upper and lower rails includes a $\frac{1}{2}$" long tenon on each end. Cut the tenons on both rails. All the tenons are $\frac{1}{4}$" thick by $\frac{1}{2}$" long and are centered on the rail ends. A stacked dado head cutter on your table saw is the best tool to form these tenons.

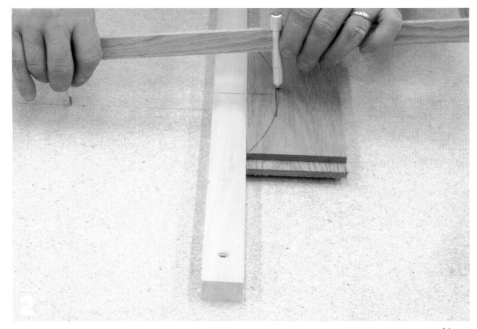

Draw an arc on the wider upper rail, beginning and ending at each end and leaving $2\frac{1}{4}$" of wood above the arc at the center of the rail. I use an adjustable "yardstick" compass that's available at most woodworking stores. The arc will have a radius that is determined by the rail width (see chapter six).

Cut the arc in the top rail using a band saw or jig saw. Leave the line visible when you cut and smooth the curve with a drum sander.

The grooves on the stiles and bottom straight rail should be $\frac{1}{2}$" deep and $\frac{1}{4}$" wide. To cut the groove in the arched top rail I've used a wing or slot cutter in my router table. Door-frame parts are safely held, and routered, in my shop-made jig, detailed below. If your cutter is like mine, you'll need to flip the rail to get a $\frac{1}{4}$"-wide groove that will be $\frac{1}{2}$" deep. The other parts grooved on the table saw are $\frac{1}{2}$" deep as well.

The $\frac{1}{4}$" plywood center panel should be cut before beginning the door assembly. The simplest method of determining the correct arc for the center panel is to dry fit the door frame with the panel in the stiles and lower rail. I've left the panel long on top. Lightly trace the inside profile of your upper rail on the panel with the rail held $\frac{7}{16}$" above the top edges of the stiles. Use a band saw or jig saw to cut the arc in the panel.

55

6

Dry fit the door assembly. Once all the parts fit properly without any undue force required, apply glue to the mortise and tenons. Clamp the door assembly and make sure that the door is square before the adhesive sets.

VARIATIONS OF THE ARCHED DOOR

Double-arched doors can be made using two wide rails. Prepare two identical rails and install one on the top and bottom of the door.

As discussed earlier, the stile and rail width of $2\frac{1}{4}$" is my own preference. Some woodworkers like wider frame pieces. You can also make the arched top rail $3\frac{1}{2}$" or $3\frac{3}{4}$" for a more dramatic curve. It's a matter of personal taste, so I suggest you use some of your scrap wood to experiment with different widths to get a style that suits your taste.

Building successful arched doors is simply a matter of keeping one rule in mind: Keep the rail height at the center of the rail above the arc equal to the width of your straight stiles and rails. If you maintain that dimension, all the doors on a project will appear as a set, no matter their width.

SHOP TALK *Cathedral Doors*

The cathedral-style frame-and-panel door is a variation on the arched frame and panel. All the construction steps are identical except the design of the curved rail(s).

Prepare the stock as for the arched door style and cut the upper rail as shown in the drawing. The rail tenons are cut before the curve, so the flat edges on both sides of the rail can be used to guide the stock on the table saw.

In this design, dimension A, which is the width of the straight run at the ends of the rail, is one-half the stile width. The material above the arc, dimension B, on the rail equals the stile width. The arc radius can be changed by altering the width of A, but keep B equal to the stile width and the door will look balanced.

Maintaining A at half the stile width and B equal to the stile width means that the radius of the arc changes for different door widths. However, all doors used for the same project, such as a cabinet doors for a kitchen, will look consistent if dimensions A and B are identical on all the doors.

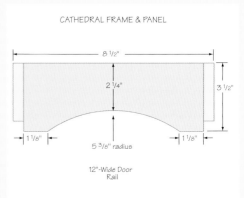

CATHEDRAL FRAME & PANEL

12"-Wide Door Rail

Building Cathedral Frame-and-Panel Doors

This example door is 12" wide and 18" high. I'm using $\frac{3}{4}$"-thick stock for the stiles and rails with a $\frac{1}{4}$"-thick veneer plywood panel. All stock used for the doors is $\frac{3}{4}$" thick. Cut two stiles at $2\frac{1}{4}$" wide by 18" long and one upper rail at $3\frac{1}{4}$" high by $8\frac{1}{2}$" wide. The bottom rail is $2\frac{1}{4}$" high by $8\frac{1}{2}$" wide. Note the width of the upper and lower rails include a $\frac{1}{2}$"-long tenon on each end. Form the tenons on both rails using a stacked dado blade on the table saw. All the tenons are $\frac{1}{4}$" thick by $\frac{1}{2}$" long and centered on the rail ends.

Draw an arc on the wider upper rail but remember to begin and end the radius $1\frac{1}{8}$" short of each end as shown on the drawing. The arc will have a radius that is determined by the rail width (see chapter six).

Cut the arc in the top rail using a band saw or jig saw. Leave the line visible when you cut and smooth the curve with a drum sander.

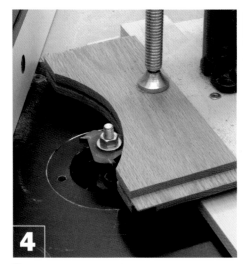

The ¼"-plywood center panel should be cut before beginning the door assembly. The simplest method of determining the correct cathedral profile for the center panel is to dry fit the door frame with the panel in the stiles and lower rail. I've left the panel long on top. Lightly trace the inside profile of your upper rail on the panel with the rail held ⁷⁄₁₆" above the top edges of the stiles. Use a band saw or jig saw to cut the profile on the panel.

The grooves in the stiles and lower straight rail should be ½" deep and ¼" wide and cut on the table saw. To cut the groove in the arched top rail, I've used a wing or slot cutter in my router table as detailed for the arched door rail. Refer to the Shop Talk on the next page about building and using the curve routing jig.

Dry fit the door assembly. Once all the parts fit properly without any undue force, apply glue to the mortise and tenons. Clamp the door assembly and make sure that the door is square before the adhesive sets.

SHOP TALK *Building a Curve Routing Jig*

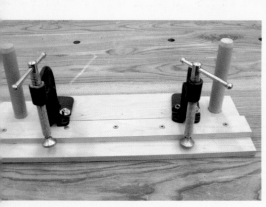

I'm not comfortable holding small curved pieces of wood when cutting grooves or profiles on the router table. My hands are too close to the cutter and have very little protection should the work piece jam or kick out.

I built this simple routing sled jig that clamps the work piece and provides handles that are well back from the router bit. It's easy to build as you can see from the picture. Use two pieces of ½"-thick plywood, one that is narrower than the other, and attach wood dowels for the handles and a couple of screw or toggle clamps. The hardware is available at many woodworking stores.

I like this jig because it lets me get a good, full grip, with both hands, to control the work piece. If a problem does occur, I'm behind the work piece. You can see how the pieces of wood are clamped in the illustrations for building arched and cathedral doors.

Raised Panel Doors

5

I've sandwiched this chapter between the chapter on flat panel doors and the next on cope-and-stick doors because raised panels can be used with all these doors. There are a number of techniques that can be used to "raise" a solid wood panel, so I will try to describe as many as possible. Use the method that best suits the equipment you have in your shop.

Raised panels begin their life as solid-wood glue-ups. The Shop Talk on the next page will describe another way to create stable solid-wood panels. If you have a jointer, the process is straightforward; it is explained in the Shop Talk section. If you don't own one of these machines, use the table saw technique described in chapter three in the section titled Solid-Wood Slab Doors.

SHOP TALK *Creating Panel Glue-ups*

Use a jointer to flatten one face of each board that will be joined.

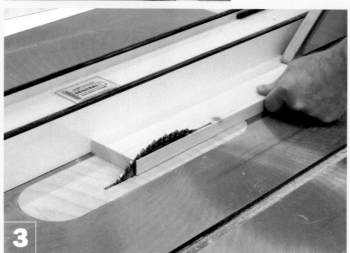

The flat face of the board should be held tightly to the jointer fence, which is set at a 90° angle to the jointer table. Push one edge through the jointer until it is smooth. That edge should now be at a 90° angle to the previously flattened face.

Place the face that was flattened on the jointer on the saw table. The jointed edge should be held tightly to the table saw fence and the opposite edge run through the saw blade. This cut will create two parallel edges that are at a 90° angle to the previously jointed face.

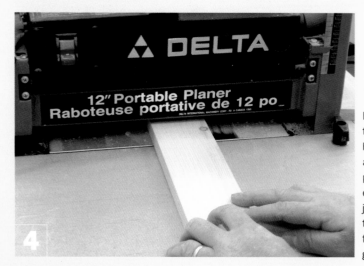

Finally, place the board's flat edge on the planer table, then dress the opposite face smooth. These four steps will provide you with a board that has flat, straight edges, that are parallel to each other and at 90° angles to the board's faces. The flat faces will also be parallel to each other. This board is now ready to be joined to other similarly prepared boards. The machined edges are butt-joined with glue and clamped until the adhesive sets. Don't over-tighten the clamps or the glue will be forced out and the joints will fail. Once the adhesive sets, you will have perfectly joined, flat, glued-up solid-wood panels.

Tapered Raised Panels

The first step in making these raised panels on a table saw is the building of a jig that will allow you to safely and accurately cut the panels. This jig can be built using any sheet material, but I prefer low-cost ³⁄₄"-thick medium-density fiberboard (MDF). It's a simple jig that's safe to use and one that improves the accuracy of your cuts.

Cut a piece of ³⁄₄" MDF 20" square. Drill three ¹⁄₂"-diameter holes in the middle of this panel, spaced evenly across the panel's width.

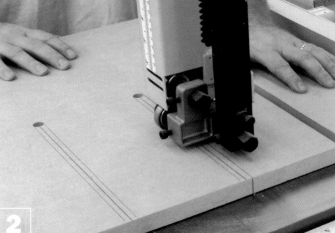

Draw lines extending each hole's outside diameter to one end of the panel. Cut the slots on a band saw or with a hand-held jig saw.

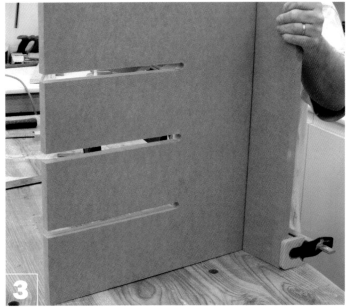

Cut a second piece of MDF at 20" long and equal to the width of your fence (see Shop Tip on the next page). Attach it to the main panel using glue and 1¹⁄₂" long screws. It should be located so that it rests on top of the fence when the lower edge of the main panel is lightly touching the table on your saw.

61

SHOP TIP

My General table saw is equipped with a square tube-style fence. Many table saws have a fence similar to this, but the width is slightly different. Delta table saw fences are different because they have a groove, that tracks on a square piece of metal, so the fence can be adjusted to the front or rear of the table.

The jig will ride on the square tube fences by using a simple box form as shown in the following steps. Delta fences require an extra cleat, cut to fit for the groove at the top backside of the fence, so it will track along the fence without slipping. With a little trial and error, you can build a custom jig for the style of fence on your own saw.

Attach a skirt board with glue and 1½"-long screws so the jig will track along the fence. It should slide freely without any side movement.

A hardwood handle should be attached to the back end of the jig. This handle allows the operator to grip the jig and safely control the feed rate. Use glue and screws to secure the handle.

A glued-up panel can now be safely raised on the table saw with the jig. The slots make it possible to clamp the panel tightly to the jig on the top edge. Set the table saw blade at a 10° angle and push each edge of the panel through the blade. Adjust the blade to cut an angled slice off each edge, leaving the outside edges ³⁄₁₆" thick to fit in the ¼"-wide stile and rail grooves. Once all the edges are cut, sand the raised panel smooth.

Table-Saw Coved Raised Panels: Version 1

Completely lower the table saw blade and clamp a board across the table top. It should be fixed so it aligns at a 90° angle to the blade and crosses it at the center. Turn on the saw and raise the blade $\frac{1}{16}$" above the table top. Push each edge of a glued-up panel across the blade using a slow, even feed rate. After all four edges have been cut, raise the blade and repeat the process. Use a push pad and be aware of the open, unguarded blade as you feed the panel.

Repeat step one until the panel edges are reduced to $\frac{3}{16}$" or to a thickness that will allow the panel to fit snugly but not tightly into the grooves of your stiles and rails. Sand the cove cut smooth. Slow, even panel feeding, taking a little material with each pass, will produce smooth cuts and eliminate a lot of sanding.

Table-Saw Coved Raised Panels: Version 2

Lower the blade before clamping a board on the table saw at approximately a 30° angle to the saw blade. Experiment with different angles between board and blade to achieve a cove profile that suits you; there isn't a "set" position for this procedure. Raise the blade $^{1}/_{16}$" and push all four edges of the glued-up panel along the fence board. Slow, steady passes will produce the smoothest cuts. After all four edges have been cut, repeat the cutting steps, raising the blade $^{1}/_{16}$".

Continue cutting until the panel edges are $^{3}/_{16}$" thick. Notice that I have created a ridge or bump in the middle of my cove cut. This is another technique you can use, which is achieved by stopping the saw and repositioning the board fence when you are about halfway through the cove. Again, I suggest you experiment with scrap material to get a cove style that suits your project.

ROUTER-TABLE RAISED PANELS

Raised center panels can be quickly and easily cut on a router table using raised-panel router bits. There are dozens of cutter styles from just as many manufacturers, but I suggest you invest in the best bits available.

Both vertical and horizontal position cutters are available; I prefer the horizontal style. I'm more comfortable raising a board's edge with these large bits when the panel is flat on the router table. Remember to use all the safety accessories with your table and fence because these are large router bits and you are milling a lot of material with each pass. Most are equipped with a guide bearing, but I still use the fence, aligned slightly behind the bearing so it becomes the primary guide, as an added safety precaution. In addition, I use only $^{1}/_{2}$"-diameter shank bits for panel raising.

You can purchase quite a few cut-

ting profiles. I have plain and ogee cutters as well as a panel-raising bit with a back cutter. I'll explain the back cutting bit later in this chapter.

Plain-Profile Panel-Raising Cutters

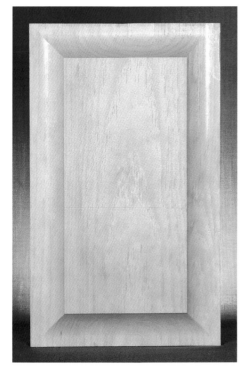

There are many plain panel-raising router bits, but the most common is a simple cove style. These bits have long, medium and short radius cuts, so you'll have to decide which profile best suits your needs.

This group of plain panel-raising bits also includes tapered cutters, which are available in a few different profiles. These bits can be used to make door center panels that can be used with many furniture styles, so it's probably the best one to purchase for general use.

Install the panel-raising bit in your router, making certain that it's properly seated and tightly locked in the chuck. Your table should be equipped with a router that's rated at 2 horsepower or more. Many woodworkers maintain that only variable-speed routers should be used because these bits seem to cut better when the router is set at one-half or three-quarter speed. There's a lot of truth in that belief, but I have successfully used fixed-speed routers to raise my panels. Experiment with router speed and panel feed rates to achieve clean cuts. However, even the correct speed and feed rates may not guarantee success; some types of wood, such as oak or maple, tend to splinter or tear out in chunks, so a lot of testing may be necessary.

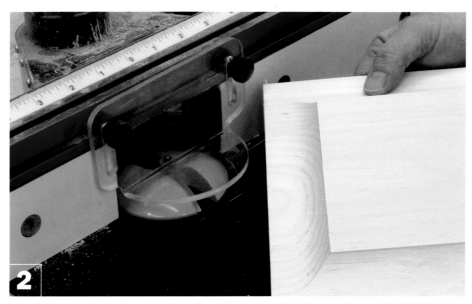

It's often better to make a number of small passes rather than on large cut with these cove panel-raising bits. Mill the end grain first, as that's where most of the tear-out occurs; then follow up with cuts along the grain. Continue making the cutting passes until the panel edges are $1/16$" thick, or the proper thickness for stile and rail frame grooves.

Figured-Profile Panel-Raising Cutters

1

The milling steps and procedures for the figured bits are the same as those for the simple plain bits. Make a number of small passes and test the cuts on scrap material before making the final cuts on the panels.

Figured panel-raising bits cut a pattern into glued-up panels. I'm using one of the more common styles, an ogee bit. However, there are many variations of this profile and more that have greater detail.

Figured bits are often chosen to match cope-and-stick bit sets, which are used to cut tenons, grooves and patterns on the edges of door-stile members and the ends of door rails. You'll find pattern styles called Roman Ogee, Classic Bead, Classic Frame and so on for both stile-and-rail bit sets as well as the panel-raising bit.

2

The panel should be guided by a bearing on the bit using a medium feed rate to achieve smooth cuts. A certain amount of finish sanding will always be required, but you can minimize it by testing for the best feed rate and router speed.

Raised-Panel Bits with Back Cutter

These special bits are available in many of the standard profiles but are also equipped with a rear cutting blade. The back cutter forms a rabbet cut on the rear face of the panel as the face is profiled. This rear cut positions the door so the front face of the frame and panel are on the same level. For more information about panel levels in a frame, refer to the Shop Talk section following these steps.

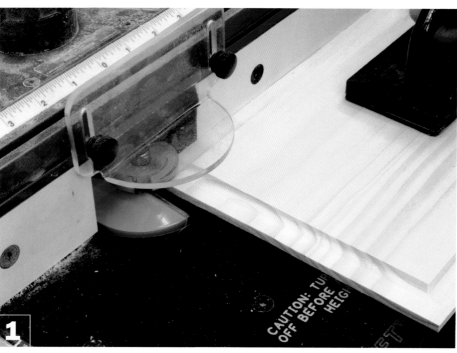

Both front and rear faces of the raised panel are milled during a cutting pass. The double-profile cut means that a panel must be raised with only one pass per edge. There's a lot of material being removed on each pass, so be sure your router bit is sharp; also test the feed rate as well as the router speed with scrap material before you begin.

Typically, a guide bearing controls the cut depth, but I always set up my router-table fence slightly behind the bearing's front face as a safety device. The bearing is the primary control, but the fence prevents the panel from being kicked back in case of a jam. With all these cutters, dust is a major concern, so a good vacuum system is necessary.

SHOP TALK   *Raised Panel vs. Door Frame Position*

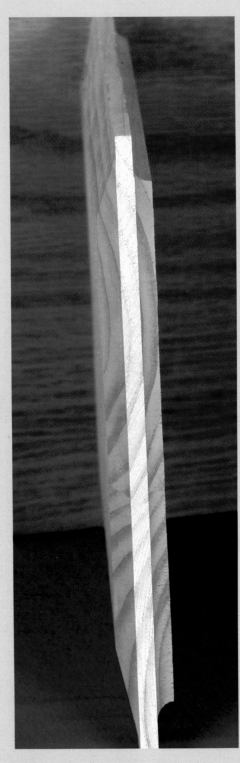

This illustration shows the edge profile on a panel that was milled with a raised-panel bit equipped with a back cutting blade. It has a specific purpose that is best explained by studying a raised panel's relationship to the front surface of a door frame.

Door frames, made with two stiles and rails, have a groove in the center to hold a flat or raised panel. The stile and rail grooves can be cut on a table saw or by using a cope-and-stick bit set (see the following chapter).

These stile and rail grooves are normally centered on the edges, which means that a raised panel of the same original thickness ($\frac{3}{4}$"-thick door-frame material and $\frac{3}{4}$"-thick raised panels) as the frame will be $\frac{1}{4}$" higher than the front face of the stiles and rails. The panel is said to be "proud of the frame" because it's held in the groove, which is $\frac{1}{4}$" in from the frame's back edge.

If you don't mind having a raised center panel proud of the frame, then there isn't a problem. If you want the center panel's front face to be on the same level as the door frame's face, you have two options. First, you can use $\frac{7}{8}$"-thick material for the stiles and rails and $\frac{5}{8}$"-thick material for the center panel. The $\frac{1}{4}$" difference, because the panel is in the grooves that are $\frac{1}{4}$" above the frame's back face, is accounted for by the thinner panel material.

The other option is to use the same thickness material for the door frame and raised center panel, but you must use a panel-raising bit equipped with a back cutting blade. The center panel's back face will have a $\frac{1}{4}$" rabbet, which will lower and level its position with respect to the frame's front face. Simply put, we would remove $\frac{1}{4}$" from the back of the panel edges so the panel would be recessed $\frac{1}{4}$" from the front surface of the door frame.

Cope-and-Stick Doors

Cope-and-stick doors are much like the tenon-and-groove doors described in chapter four. The "tenon" is made with a cope bit and the "groove" on the rail and stile edges are made with a matching stick bit. They are a little more detailed than the simple tenon-into-a-groove design, but only because there are a few added cutting profiles on the bit sets.

These doors can be fitted with a ¼"-thick flat panel as shown in chapter four, or with one of the raised panels described in chapter five. The panels are held in the "stick" or groove cut by a router bit in a router table. I don't suggest trying to use these bits freehand in a router because they are quite large and remove a considerable amount of material. I recommend using a good router, rated at 2 or more horsepower, and a solid router table. And even then, be sure to follow the safety recommendations explained this chapter.

COPE-AND-STICK BIT SETS

There are normally two bits in a rail-and-stile cutter set. The inside edges of the rails and stiles are cut with a stick bit and the rail ends are formed to fit the stick cuts with a cope bit. There are a number of different patterns available, much like the panel-raising bits, including plain, ogee, coved and so on.

I prefer a bit set rather than the single rail-and-stile combination bit that has removable cutters for repositioning when each profile is cut. I would also suggest that you use $\frac{1}{2}$"-diameter shank bits in a router capable of taking a $\frac{1}{2}$" shaft, because these bits will come under a great deal of stress.

SHOP TALK *Calculating Cope-and-Stick Door Sizes*

Take a look at the cutting profile in this illustration. You'll see the tenon-into-a-groove arrangement created by the cutting bits. Each bit set cuts a little differently, so you'll have to calculate how much extra length is required on the rails to produce the final door size required.

Door height is equal to stile length so, if I require an 18" high door, my stiles will be 18" long. The rail width is another matter because the cope cutter is removing material to form the tenon. The bit set I'm using requires an added $\frac{7}{8}$" to the rail length to get the desired door width.

For example, the door I need is 12" wide by 18" high. My stile and rail width is $2\frac{1}{4}$" so that width is doubled (for two stiles); subtracting that figure from the required final door width of 12" gives me a rail length of $7\frac{1}{2}$". However, for my bit set, I know that an additional $\frac{7}{8}$" must be added to the rail length to account for the material removed in cutting. Your bit set will likely be different, so test your measurements on scrap material before you begin making doors to get the waste factor number.

Test the bit set and make a sample pattern for the stile-and-rail cutter. Keep those patterns handy so the bits can be aligned for cutting. It will save a lot of set-up time.

Square Cope-and-Stick Doors

Square cope-and-stick doors are the simplest form of this door style. They are formed with a bit set that cuts tenons and grooves. The process is similar to the tenon-and-groove doors in chapter four but the patterns are more detailed because of the bit profiles that are used.

Set up your bit set with samples, determine the "adding" factor for rail lengths, and cut the parts to size based on the calculations described in the Shop Talk on calculating door sizes.

Cut the stile and rail parts to size. Cope the ends of each rail with a backer board behind the wood to minimize tear-out. Notice that I'm making the cope cuts first. Some woodworkers prefer this method while others cut the stick profile first. I don't feel one way is superior to the other; I often cut my stick profiles before the rail-end cope cuts. Experiment with both methods to find the procedure that works best for you.

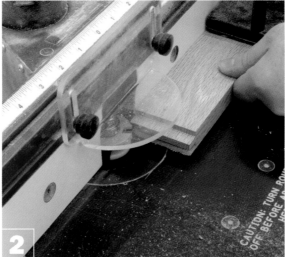

Once the rails have been coped, cut the stick profile on the inside edge of both rails and stiles. Before making the final cut, set up the stick bit and use scrap lumber of the same thickness as the rails to match the previously cut coped rails to the new stick setup.

Dry fit the door frame and measure the inside dimensions. My groove, or stick cut, depth for the bit set I'm using is $\frac{7}{16}$". I want to leave a little room for panel and frame expansion and contraction, so I'll add $\frac{3}{4}$" ($\frac{7}{16}$" plus $\frac{7}{16}$" minus $\frac{1}{8}$") to the inside height and width of the frame.

Cut the center panel to size. At this point you have two options; you can install a ¼"-thick veneer plywood center panel as shown, or a raised solid-wood panel like the ones described in chapter five.

Raised center panels begin as solid-wood glue-ups. The boards can be prepared on a table saw as explained in chapter three or by using a jointer and planer as described in chapter five.

Raise the panel using a panel-raising router bit. Or, you can use one of the table saw methods described in chapter five.

To reduce door panel "rattle" (because it will be loose in the frame) install small strips of soft foam in the groove. I use strips cut from a roll of soft weatherstripping material that I purchase at my local hardware store. These large rolls of foam are used to insulate doors and are commonly available as well as inexpensive. One roll of weatherstripping will be enough to do dozens of doors. You can also buy any of the commercial products made for this application from your local woodworking store.

Assemble the door by applying glue to the cope cuts only. Clamp the door frame and measure the diagonals to be sure they are equal, which means that the door is square. Do not glue the panel in place so it and the frame members can move as humidity levels change.

SHOP TALK *Calculating the Radius for Arched and Cathedral Doors*

The radius of an arc for arched and cathedral doors can be calculated mathematically. First, you must understand that a line between two points on a circle is called a chord. The arc on both cathedral and arched doors is part of a circle, and the chord is the straight line between the arc ends that meet the bottom edge of the rail.

In the equation, the chord dimension is shown as C and the height of the arc at its center point is H. The formula states that the chord C is squared (multiplied by itself) and four times the height dimension squared is added to that number. The number is then divided by a figure that is eight times the height. The result is the radius of the circle in inches and indicates the spread between point and pencil on a beam or large compass.

For example, an arched door upper rail is 16" wide. Because the arc is drawn between both ends of a rail, the chord is equal to the rail width or 16". The formula states that the chord is squared (16 x 16 = 256) and a figure of four times the height of the arc at the center, squared, is added to that number (4 x 4 = 16). The value is 272, which is divided by eight times the height (8 x 1 = 8) or eight. The answer is 34" (272 divided by 8), which is the radius of the circle.

Set a beam compass at 34" from point to pencil, and place the point on a center line extended through the arc. The pencil is set 1" above the rail bottom. Draw the arc for an arched door or follow the same procedure for a cathedral door.

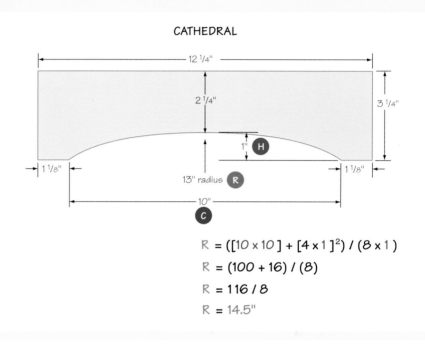

CATHEDRAL

$$R = ([10 \times 10] + [4 \times 1]^2) / (8 \times 1)$$
$$R = (100 + 16) / (8)$$
$$R = 116 / 8$$
$$R = 14.5"$$

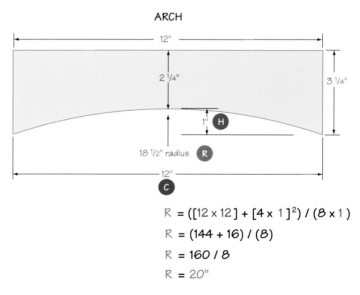

ARCH

$$R = ([12 \times 12] + [4 \times 1]^2) / (8 \times 1)$$
$$R = (144 + 16) / (8)$$
$$R = 160 / 8$$
$$R = 20"$$

Arch Cope-and-Stick Door

The arched cope-and-stick door is a variation of the square door. The upper rail, and sometimes both rails, has an arc pattern. The upper rail is wider because material will be removed when cutting the arc.

Maintaining fixed dimensions on all arched doors, particularly those for a project such as kitchen cabinets, makes all the doors appear similar no matter what their width. Refer to chapter four for more details on maintaining visual consistency in arched rail doors.

1 Cut all the parts to size. I usually cut straight rails and stiles 2¼" wide and arched rails at 3¼" wide. Draw the arc on the curved rails.

2 Use a band saw or jig saw to cut the arc. Sand the curve smooth.

3 Cope the rail ends. Remember to keep the rails oriented the same way when cutting — don't flip them. In other words, keep the same face up when you turn the rail to cut the opposite end. Use a backer board to minimize tear-out.

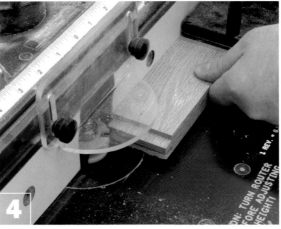

4 Change to the stick bit, align and test the bit for a correct cutting pattern, then cut the straight stiles and rail.

5 The curved upper rail edge requires a stick cut. Use a push pad and carefully enter the cutter. Most router bits spin counterclockwise in a table, so the wood can be pushed backwards and onto the leading face of the bit. Hold the board securely and enter the bit's cutting path carefully. Notice that my router fence is set slightly behind the bit to act as a backstop should the work piece be thrown back. Use care and all safety devices when cutting the curved rails.

6 The center panel can be a ¼" thick piece of plywood veneer or a solid-wood raised panel. The simplest method to determine panel size is to lay the door frame on the panel and trace inside the frame. Notice that my upper curved rail is ³⁄₈" higher in the door frame than normal. This will allow me to draw the correct cut line for the curve, which will properly sit in the ⁷⁄₁₆"-deep groove made by the stick router bit.

7 Prepare the panel of your choice. Raising curved panels with a router bit is fairly easy as long as you push the panel smoothly through the bit and keep it tight to the bearing.

8 Apply glue to the rail ends and assemble the door. Clamp the door frame and make sure that it's square.

Cathedral Cope-and-Stick Door

Cut all the parts to size. I usually cut straight rails and stiles 2¼" wide and arched rails at 3¼" wide. Draw the arc on the rails, leaving 1⅛" of straight rail on either side of the arc. The arc rise at its center point is 1"; the radius formula can be used to determine the compass setting.

Cathedral-style cope-and-stick doors are a variation of the arched door. The arc is shorter, leaving equally dimensioned straight lengths of the rail at either end. The combination of straight and arched cuts in the rail distinguishes the cathedral style. These doors are referred to by other names but to save confusion I'll refer to them as cathedral doors.

Once again, a router stick bit will be tracked in a curve, so exercise caution and follow the previous suggestions about safe practices. If you'd prefer not to get too close to the bit with a push pad, use the curved router jig. Always wear safety glasses and hearing protection, and keep the router-table fence as close as possible to the bit as a safety precaution.

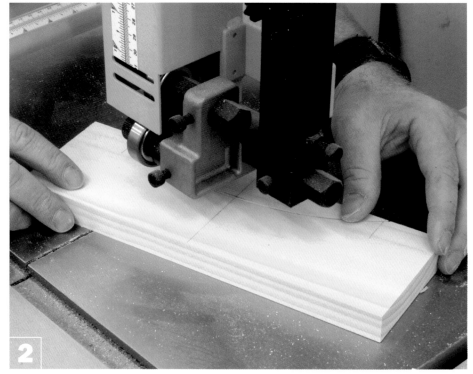

Use a band saw or jig saw to cut the arc. Sand the curve smooth.

Cope the rail ends. Remember to keep the rails oriented the same way when cutting — don't flip them. In other words, keep the same face up when you turn the rail to cut the opposite end. Use a backer board to minimize tear-out.

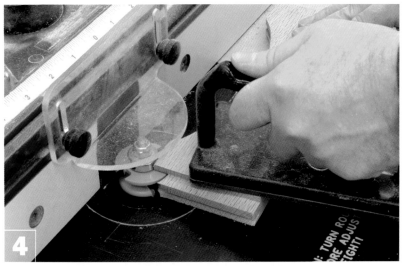

Change to the stick bit, align and test the bit for a correct cutting pattern, then cut the straight stiles and rail. The curved upper rail edge requires a stick cut as well. Use a push pad and carefully enter the cutter. Most router bits spin counterclockwise in a table, so the wood can be pushed backwards and onto the leading face of the bit. Hold the board securely and enter the bit's cutting path carefully. Once again, notice that my router fence is set slightly behind the bit to act as a backstop should the work piece be thrown back. Use care and all safety devices when cutting the curved rails.

The center panel can be a ¼"-thick piece of plywood veneer or a solid-wood raised panel. The simplest method to determine panel size is to lay the door frame on the panel and trace inside the frame. As with the arched door, notice that my upper curved rail is ⅜" higher in the door frame than normal. This will allow me to draw the correct cut line for the curve, which will properly sit in the $\frac{7}{16}$"-deep groove made by the stick router bit.

Prepare the panel of your choice. Push the panel smoothly through the bit and keep it tight to the bearing. Apply glue to the rail end and assemble the door. Clamp the door frame and make sure that it's square.

Glass Door Frames

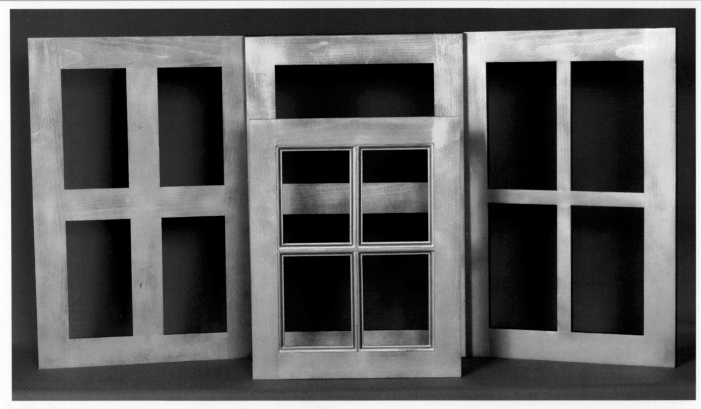

Wood door frames that are built to hold glass panels are often referred to as glass door frames. While glass is the most common type of insert, there are many other options for these frames. In place of a wood or glass center panel, consider decorative plastic, thin metal sheets or leaded glass for your next project.

I've seen many beautiful and creative frame-door panels. Hammered copper sheets are a dramatic change of pace when compared to plain glass or wood. How about using textured, colored plastic sheets, or any of the many art glass products such as those with a frosted or etched finish? You can add a lot of visual interest to your project by using a decorative panel in a wooden door frame.

Table-Saw Frames

Door frames can be made quickly and easily on a table saw. This style of door tends to be a little bulky in appearance and is best suited for Mission or Shaker-style projects. The stiles and rails are my 2¼" wide standard size, so hidden hinges can be used. If you plan on using more traditional North American-style hinges, however, you can lighten the appearance by using narrower stiles and rails.

These doors are made with tenon-and-groove joinery, explained previously in this book. However, they will be fitted with decorative panels in place of the wood panels or ¼"-plywood centers. The panels must be easy to remove in case of breakage and many of these doors will have muntins (dividers), so a couple of design changes are necessary.

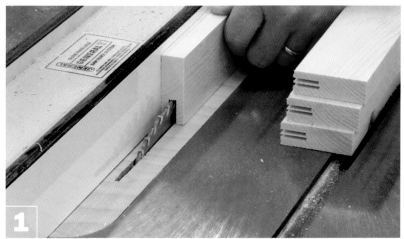

Cut all the parts needed to make this door frame, which will be 24" high by 16" wide using ¾"-thick stock. The two stiles are 2¼" wide by 24" long and the three rails 2¼" wide by 13" long. Set the saw blade ¾" above the table and the fence ¼" from the blade. Run each piece through the blade and then reverse the feed direction on the next pass to center the groove. The center muntin needs a groove on each long edge; the stiles and rails require a groove on one edge only. There may be some material left in the center of the groove. If so, reset the fence and make a clean-out pass on each piece. The amount of material left in the middle depends on the thickness of your saw blade.

The three rails need a ¼"-thick by ¾"-long tenon centered on each end. The tenons can be cut in a number of ways, as previously explained but a dado blade on a table saw seems to be the most efficient method.

SHOP NOTE

Many woodworkers prefer to pin the tenons with ⅝" brad nails. You can use this technique on many door styles. The pins hold the joints until the glue sets, so it's a helpful technique if you don't have a lot of clamps.

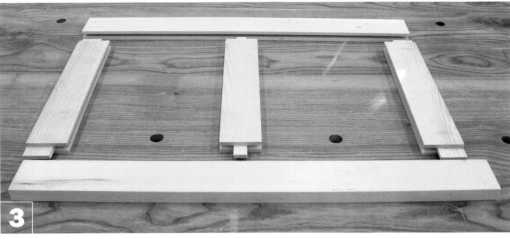

3

You should have two stiles with grooves on the inside edge and three rails with tenons and grooves, as shown in the photograph. Note that the middle rail, or muntin, has a groove on each long edge as well as a tenon on each end.

4

Brush glue on the tenons and assemble the frame. Center the muntin and make sure that the door frame is square before the adhesive sets up.

5

The next step is to cut away half the groove material on the back edge using a ⅜" rabbet bit in a router. Square the corners after routing.

6

Install the glass or decorative center panel. To stop center-panel rattle, I use soft foam weatherstripping that is sold in long rolls. The roll can be cut into 1" long strips and inserted in the grooves before installing the panels. The foam strips work very well and are inexpensive.

7

This door style has a heavy appearance, so I typically round over the outside profile with a $\frac{3}{8}$"-radius router bit. This step is optional, but you may prefer the softer look; so try a couple of sample profiles, including a cove edge, to find one that suits your taste.

SHOP NOTE

You can purchase rubber gasket material for glass doors that have a groove setup like the one shown on this door frame. The groove is $\frac{3}{4}$" deep but half the back edge has been removed, so the teeth on this gasket material fit in the remaining half and the rubber secures the glass. Rubber gasket material is hard to find in some areas, so small brad nails, triangle glazing points, glazing putty or silicone adhesive caulk can be used to secure the glass instead.

81

Divided Four-Light Doors

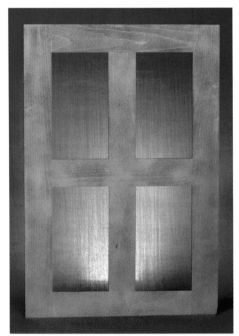

You can easily create glass door frames with multiple *lights* (sections) for panels — it's simply a matter of adding muntins. Like the center muntin shown in the previous project, each must have grooves on both long edges as well as tenons on each end.

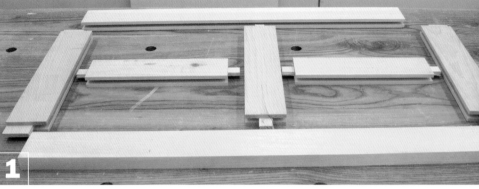

1 Follow the previous construction steps for table-saw frame doors. The upper and lower sections are divided by vertical muntins, which transforms the frame into a four-light door. Vertical muntin dimensions equal rail-to-rail distances plus 1½" for the tenons on either end. Like the horizontal muntin, the vertical version must also be grooved on both long edges. The photo illustrates a partial layout before assembly.

2 Repeat the assembly steps of applying glue to the tenons only and clamping the door frame until the adhesive sets up. The back can be routed with a ⅜" rabbet router bit and the panels installed using one of the options mentioned in the previous project.

Mortise-and-Tenon Frame Glass Doors

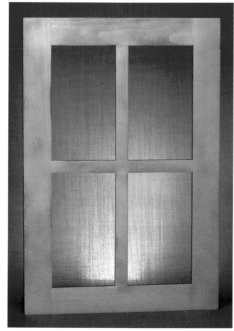

For those that prefer traditional-style joinery, this mortise-and-tenon decorative-panel door frame should interest you. The corner joints, as well as the muntins, are secured using this type of joint.

Glass or decorative panels rest behind the muntins, so a thinner and therefore lighter-looking frame can be built. Tenons can be cut by hand or by using a number of methods previously explained in this book. In addition, the mortises can be drilled out and squared with a chisel or cut on a dedicated mortising machine such as the one shown in the construction steps. It doesn't matter how the parts are machined as long as the end result is a well-formed mortise-and-tenon joint.

Cut the stiles and rails to size for a door that's 24" high by 16" wide. You will require two stiles at ¾" wide by 2¼" thick by 24" long and two rails that are ¾" thick by 2¼" wide by 13" long. The 13"-long rail includes enough material to form a ¾"-long by ¼"-thick tenon on both ends. Cut the parts to size and form the rail tenons with one added step: These doors will have blind mortise-and-tenon joints, meaning that the joint won't be visible on the door ends. This is accomplished by cutting ¼" off each tenon edge. The tenon width is reduced to 1¾" and centered on the rail end.

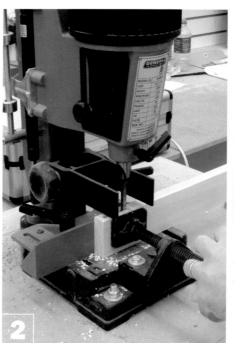

Form the ¾"-deep by ¼"-wide by 1¾"-long mortise on the inside edge of both stiles. The mortise starts ¼" away from the stile end and stops 2" from the end to make the required 1¾"-long mortise.

Dry assemble the frame. Use a ⅜" rabbet bit to cut a ¼"-deep by ⅜"-wide rabbet on the back inside face of the frame for the center panel. Square the corners after completing the rabbet cut.

These door muntins are ½" thick and 1" wide with a ¼"-thick by ½"-wide tenon on either end. Notice that the muntin tenons are offset and located ¼" back from the front face. They are ¾" long and easily formed on a table saw fitted with a standard blade.

If your door has vertical and horizontal muntins, a dado must be cut on each piece where they cross to create a half-lap joint. Be careful to orient the dado cuts correctly because they will have to be positioned on the back of one muntin and the front of the other at the intersection. The dado cuts are half the thickness of the muntin thickness and equal to their width. These can also be formed on a table saw.

The simplest way to locate the mortises on the door frame for the muntin tenons is to lay the grid on the dry-assembled door frame. Mark the tenon positions by tracing their outline on the door-frame face.

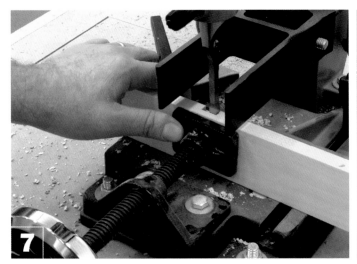

Form the mortises in the frame rails and stiles. Keep in mind that they are set back ¼" from the door-frame face to properly receive the muntin tenons.

The door frame can now be assembled with glue on all the tenons. It's a bit like a jigsaw puzzle to put all the parts together, so practice with a few dry runs before beginning the final assembly.

Cope-and-Stick Frame Doors

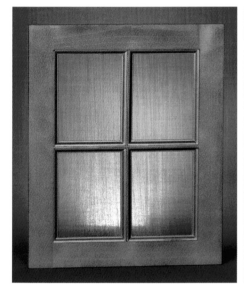

Most cope-and-stick bit sets can be configured to cut door frames for glass and decorative panels. The manufacturer provides instructions for changing and repositioning. Generally, the stick or rail-and-stile edge-cutting bit is set up to make the standard front profile and a full rabbet cut on the back face. The cope or rail end-cutting bit is changed to produce a full tenon that rests in the stile rabbet cut.

1 Change the cutters on your cope-and-stick bits for a glass door profile. Test the cutting profile on the stick bit to get a sample profile that can be used to check the alignment of the cope cutter. Run rail-end test pieces through the cope bit until you achieve the proper profile, then cut both ends of each rail.

2 Once the cope cuts on the rail ends are complete, cut the stick profile on the inside edge of each stile and rail. You should always run test pieces through these bits after installing them to make sure the correct profile is cut. Dry fit the stiles and rail parts to ensure the frame is cut properly.

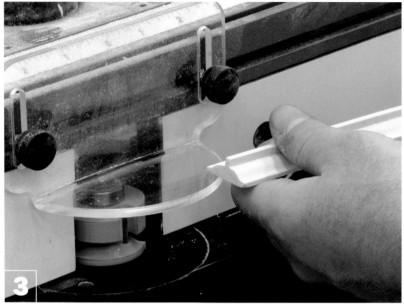

Assemble the frame using glue on the cope cuts and secure it with clamps until the adhesive sets.

Form the cope-and-stick cuts on the muntins following the steps described in the Shop Talk at the end of this section. Muntin sizes are calculated much like the rail-length calculations used for cope-and-stick doors: all the dimensions are based on uncut parts from point to point. For example, in the chapter on cope-and-stick doors I discussed bit-set profiles. To find the amount of material that must be added to the rail width with a given stile width, you must first cut a test frame.

My standard stiles are $2\frac{1}{4}$" wide, so to build a 12"-wide door my rails, without any profiles cut, should be $7\frac{1}{2}$" long (12" - $2\frac{1}{4}$" x 2 = rail length). Now, cut the $7\frac{1}{2}$" rail copes and the stile-and-rail stick profiles. Assemble the door and measure its width. My measurement is $11\frac{1}{8}$" wide after attaching the stiles to a rail. That means my cut factor with my bit set is plus $\frac{7}{8}$", which is added to the rail widths. To end up with a 12"-wide door, I'll need two $2\frac{1}{4}$"-wide stiles and two $8\frac{3}{8}$"-long rails ($7\frac{1}{2}$" plus the $\frac{7}{8}$" cut factor for my bit set).

The horizontal muntin is the same length as the rails. Vertical muntins are measured from uncut sized rails and center muntins. A 24"-high by 12"-wide door will require rails and horizontal muntins that are $8\frac{3}{8}$" long (see above). Vertical muntins, when attached to a horizontal center muntin, are $10\frac{1}{8}$" long before cutting with the cope-and-stick bits (door height 24" minus 2 times the rail width or $4\frac{1}{2}$" minus uncut the horizontal muntin width of 1", divided by 2 equals $9\frac{1}{4}$" plus the $\frac{7}{8}$" cut factor or $10\frac{1}{8}$" long).

The muntin cope cuts rest on the stick profile cuts, which are mirror images. They are secured with glue and clamped until the adhesive sets. These small muntins are delicate but they won't be supporting any weight; however, handle them carefully when they are being attached to the door frame.

SHOP TALK *Cutting Small Cope-and-Stick Muntins Safely*

Muntins used on cope-and-stick doors are small and delicate, generally 1" wide and $\frac{1}{2}$" thick. Cutting these small pieces with cope-and-stick router bits can be dangerous because they so easily shatter and split if they are not handled properly. Here's a method that will help you avoid problems when routing small parts.

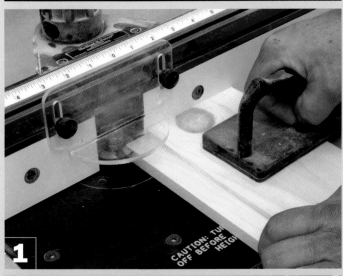

Align the router-table fence with the bearing on the cope bit so both fence and bearing guide the muntin in the same plane. Once the correct muntin length has been calculated, form the cope cuts on each end. Push the muntins through the cope bit with a wide backer board behind it. This board will provide a lot more surface area and stabilize the small muntins as they pass through the bit. Be sure the muntin is held tightly to the backer board.

Before cutting the stick profiles on the muntins, cut a cope profile into the edge of a 4"-wide piece of MDF, stopping 2" from the end. This cope profile will hold the stick profile that will be formed on one edge of the muntin.

Switch to a stick bit and form one edge profile on each muntin. After making a test cut, turn off the router and place the profiled wood edge against the stick bit. Ensure that the outfeed fence on your router table will support the reduced width of the work piece after cutting. If it doesn't align properly, shim or adjust the outfeed fence so the work piece is supported by the infeed fence before the cut and the outfeed fence after cutting. The cutter bearings should be in line with the infeed fence for this operation.

This is the point where problems arise when milling narrow muntins. Once the opposite stick profile is cut, there's very little flat material left on the muntin and it will tip on the router table — not a safe situation. The previously coped MDF jig can support the already profiled edge of the muntin so the opposite side can be cut safely. Insert the muntin in the jig and hold it securely against the router-table fence.

The muntin is secure in the jig's cope cut and trapped tightly against the router fence. It can be pushed through the bit to cut the stick profile on the opposite edge of the muntin.

Pocket, Flipper and Tambour Doors

In this chapter, we'll discuss the hardware associated with pocket and flipper doors rather than the doors themselves. Doors for these applications may be built using any of the construction styles described in previous chapters. Pocket and flipper doors are so named for their tracking hardware, which may be applied to any standard door.

There are a number of companies that manufacture pocket-door hardware. Most of them provide detailed installation instructions, but I will discuss some general principles that apply to all these hardware types. Most pocket- and flipper-door hardware systems use double ball-bearing tracks, with doors attached to the slides using European-style hidden hinges.

Tambour doors are made from wood attached to a fabric backing. They are often used for kitchen appliance garages or roll-top desks. However, tam-

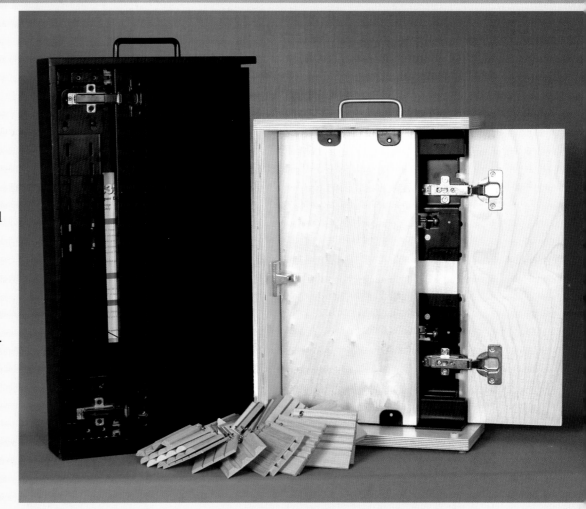

bours can also be used when front-opening space or standard door-clearance swings are restricted. Regular cabinet doors that block passageways or room traffic when fully opened can be replaced with a tambour door that rolls into the cabinet.

HARDWARE FOR POCKET AND FLIPPER DOORS

Look at the mechanics of the pocket door in this cabinet. Now imagine the same unit turned on its side: that's a flipper door. The hardware for both pocket (vertical) and flipper (horizontal) doors is the same. The only difference is the addition of roller guides in the flipper-door cabinet to hold it horizontally when pushed into the cabinet.

Pocket-door hardware is installed according to the manufacturer's instructions. Some hardware makers require that a piece of wood be cut to tie the upper and lower tracks together. Many manufacturers sell pocket-door sets for the left or right side of a cabinet. A two-door cabinet normally requires both right and left slide sets.

Most pocket door hardware can be used on doors up to 78" in height. Pocket-door hardware can be purchased in even lengths from 10" to 28". The slide length should equal the cabinet depth in most cases. Typically, slides travel about 4" to 4$\frac{1}{2}$" less than their stated length. A 22" pocket-door slide will let the door travel about 17$\frac{1}{2}$" into the cabinet. A 36" wide cabinet would have doors about 17" wide, so the cabinet depth should be designed to use 22" glides to hide as much of the door as possible. However, consider the shape of the handles or knobs that you plan to install before buying

PHOTO CREDIT: ACCURIDE CORP.

them, because they can affect door travel if they are too large.

Accuride and Blum, along with most other manufacturers whose hardware I've installed, supply detailed instructions and specifications for installing their products. The

hardware isn't difficult to install, but be aware of the issues discussed in this chapter (such as door thickness) before you design the cabinet, build the doors or buy the hardware.

Some flipper- and pocket-door sets don't require a wood connector because an adjustable metal plate is included.

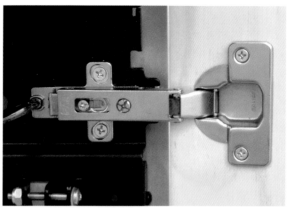

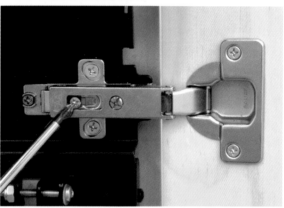

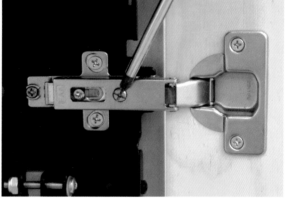

The hidden hinges that are used by many manufacturers offer adjustments to fine-tune the door location. This is the vertical adjustment, which moves the door up and down. It's used to balance the door on the cabinet and to align doors to each other.

This adjusting screw moves the door toward or away from the cabinet's front edge. Inset doors are set flush with the cabinet's front edge while overlay doors normally require a gap of ⅛" for proper operation.

The third adjusting screw is used to move the door from side to side. The door or doors can be aligned to the cabinet sides and to each other. This is an important adjusting screw to use when aligning inset cabinet doors.

Pocket and flipper doors can be inset, meaning that the door edges are flush and on the same plane as the cabinet's sides, bottom and top boards. The hardware is normally designated as inset or overlay and must be ordered specifically for your application. The latest offering is the so-called full-overlay pocket- or flipper-door hardware. Full overlay normally means the door will overlay or cover the cabinet's sides, top and bottom board. However, the term means something a little different when discussing pocket-door hardware because only the sides overlay on pocket doors. The top of the door must be slightly lower than the cabinet's top board and the bottom of the door must be slightly above the cabinet bottom board or the door can't be pushed into the cabinet. With respect to pocket doors, the term overlay means that the door covers part of the cabinet's side(s) only.

Tambour Doors

TAMBOUR DOORS

As previously mentioned, tambour doors are made with rigid slats that are attached to a cloth backing with contact cement. Wood slats can be milled with a number of different designs using a router bit, or they can be simple flat slats cut on a table saw.

Slat width should be about 1", or less, particularly when a track with many turns is being used to guide the door. The slat material is normally wood but can be plastic or any other material. Slat thickness deter-

mines track width, so it is a major consideration when designing the door. Thick, heavy and wide slats require a large track width that may not be desirable in your furniture project.

Tambour doors are relatively easy to make, but commercial versions are available at most woodworking stores. Investigate the selection and cost of tambour-door sheets in your area to determine the value of making your own. If you decide to make your own tambour sheets, here are the steps to follow.

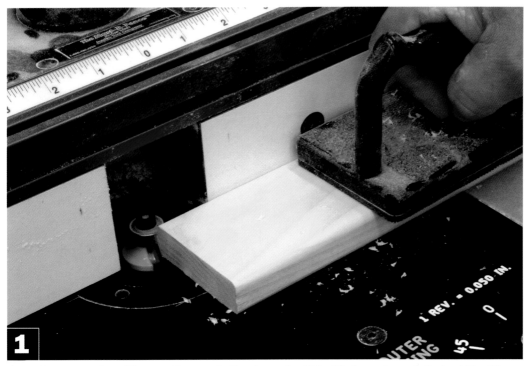

1

Start the process by milling a pattern on both edges of a 4" to 5" piece of wood. It should be 1" longer than the required finished width of your door. I'm using a ⅜" roundover bit in my router, which is mounted on a table. Both edges on each upper and lower face are being milled.

2

Rip each side of the milled board. Return to the router and form the pattern on each cut edge. Repeat the ripping step on the saw and then dress the edges once more. Keep repeating these steps until the required number of slats has been cut.

SHOP SAFETY NOTE

Cutting thin ¼" thick strips of wood on a table saw can be dangerous. It's well worth your time to build this pusher sled that rides on the table saw guide fence. My saw is equipped with a General Mfg. square-style fence, but the sled can be built to ride on just about any fence. Notice that the ¼"-thick pusher board, which is notched at the back, can guide and securely hold the wood as it travels through the blade. A featherboard to hold the material tightly against the fence should also be used in combination with the sled. These sleds are quick and easy to make and should always be used when cutting thin wood strips with the saw.

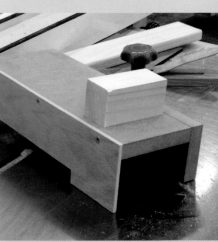

93

Tack a piece of denim tightly on a scrap sheet of wood. Denim is available at fabric stores and can be purchased by the yard. The material should be 2" to 3" wider than the required final tambour door width. Apply contact cement to the back of each slat as well as the surface of the cloth. Follow the manufacturer's directions when working with contact cement. Lay the slats on the fabric so they are in contact with each other. Use a flat board with weight on top to press the slats tightly against the cloth backing.

Once the glue has set, strap the tambour sheet to a scrap of particleboard or plywood. I use two strips of wood that are attached to the scrap material with screws. Run the panel through the table saw to create one straight edge. The panel and slats should be cut at the same time. Set the saw fence to the required finished width for your tambour door. Push the opposite edge of the panel through the saw blade with the previously dressed edge against the fence.

SHOP TALK *Tambour Door Tracks*

Tambour doors normally run in a slot cut with a router. On furniture projects such as a roll-top desk, a guide on the router is used to follow the profile of the cabinet's side panels. The track width is slightly wider than that of the tambour door slats and backing combined. The track depth is typically $\frac{1}{4}$" to $\frac{3}{8}$" deep.

Most tambour sheets have a thicker bottom board attached. This piece will act as a handle and door stop and is $\frac{1}{16}$" narrower than the inside dimension of the cabinet where the tambour door tracks. This wood bottom board keeps the tambour aligned in the tracks.

The routed-wood track is the most common guide system for tambour doors, but plastic tracks are also available. However, a project that has "hills and valleys," such as a roll-top desk, is best suited to the routed track method.

Cabinet Drawers

9

PHOTO CREDIT: CANAC KITCHENS

Drawers are required for many woodworking projects. You'll find them in desks, kitchen cabinets, storage cabinets, workshops and many more applications. We need drawers to store and organize all sorts of things in every room of the house, office and workshop.

Some woodworkers believe that a drawer lacks quality unless it's built with dovetail joinery. I don't hold that opinion. There are dozens of ways to build high-quality drawers, and all of them have a purpose and place in modern cabinetry.

I'll start by describing drawers made with melamine particleboard (PB) and then move on to other materials such as Baltic birch plywood and solid wood. I'll explain some of the joinery options as well as the hardware that can be used for your drawers.

Melamine Particleboard Drawers

Cut the sides, front, back and bottom boards to size using ⅝"-thick melamine PB. The exposed top edges as well as the side edges of the bottom board can be covered with heat-activated iron-on edge tape. Refer to the Shop Talk following this section for methods to use when determining drawer-box sizes. Join the sides to the front and back boards using biscuits, glue, and clamps or 2"-long PB screws. Always drill a pilot hole and then counterbore the hole slightly before driving any screws into the joint.

One of the most common applications for drawers and pullouts is in the kitchen. Just about every kitchen cabinet project involves drawer-building. You'll find banks of drawers, drawer-over-door cabinets and pullouts. It's not unusual to have ten or twelve drawers in the average kitchen. Often, these drawers are constructed using melamine PB and butt joinery secured with biscuits or 2"-long PB screws. The following steps outline an excellent method to use when building melamine PB drawers.

Attach the full-thickness bottom board with 2" PB screws. If the bottom board was cut square, the drawer box will be square.

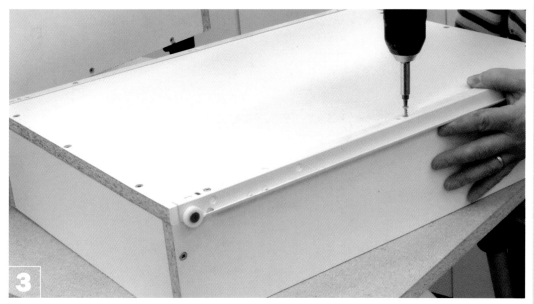

3

The drawer box can be fitted with bottom-mount drawer glides. They are aligned flush with the front edge of the box and secured with ⅝"-long screws. Standard drawer-glide sets will allow the drawers to slide out of the cabinet three-quarters of their length. They are easy to install, reliable, inexpensive, and operate smoothly on nylon-bearing wheels.

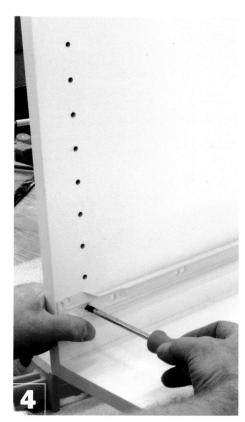

4

The cabinet runners are part of the drawer-glide set and are secured to the cabinet's sides with ⅝" screws. Set them back ⅛" from the cabinet's front edge and at 90° to that edge. Use a carpenter's square, resting on the front edge of the cabinet, to draw a reference line to help align the runners.

5

Test the drawer's operation. It should slide smoothly in and out of the cabinet and rest firmly on the runners. Push down on each front corner of the drawer to test its stability. If either front corner moves down as you press, the runners must be realigned. A "bouncing" drawer corner means that the cabinet runner on that side is too high at the back end and should be lowered slightly. Test the front corners and adjust the cabinet runners until both sit firmly on the glides.

SHOP TALK *Calculating Face-Frame Drawer Sizes*

In general, the 1" rule applies to most drawer-building projects when using modern hardware. Bottom-mounted and side-mounted slides made by manufacturers such as Blum and Accuride require a $\frac{1}{2}$" space between the outside of the drawer box and the cabinet side for proper installation and operation. Simply stated, the drawer box is 1" narrower than the cabinet's interior width.

The drawer opening is measured from inside edge to inside edge of the face frame. Subtract 1" from that dimension, which will give you the drawer box's outside width. To simplify matters, I also subtract 1" from the drawer opening height to determine my drawer box height.

This "rule" is very general, so I suggest you read the manufacturer's instructions packed with your hardware. One important issue to keep in mind if you plan to use the new hardware: most drawer-glide systems are designed to operate based on frameless-cabinet building styles. The cabinet's side is the cabinet's face and therefore the opening equals the sides' inside face-to-face dimension. But, that doesn't mean the hardware cannot be used with face frame style cabinets.

If the face frame's inside width is smaller than the cabinet's inside width, cleats or spacers must be installed to mount the glides flush with the inside of the face frame. It's a simple matter of attaching small strips of wood to mount the hardware.

SHOP TALK *Calculating Frameless Drawer Sizes*

The same 1" rule applies to most drawer-building projects when building frameless cabinet drawers. Most drawer slides require a $\frac{1}{2}$" space between the outside of the drawer box and the cabinet side for proper installation and operation.

The drawer opening is measured from the inside face of one side panel to the inside face of the opposite side panel. Subtract 1" from that dimension to determine the drawer box's outside width. This "rule" is very general, so I suggest you read the manufacturer's instructions packed with your hardware.

Calculating drawer-box heights for frameless cabinets is a little more involved. First, use the height measurement for a standard door in your project. For kitchen cabinets, a full-height base cabinet door is used as a reference. Drawer-face heights, plus the $\frac{1}{16}$" gap between them, should equal the height of base cabinet doors in the same project. A three-drawer base should have a combined drawer face and gap height equal the standard door height.

Decide on the height of each drawer face according to your requirements. For example, a three-drawer base could have two $10\frac{15}{16}$"-high bottom drawer faces and one 8"-high top drawer face, as well as two $\frac{1}{16}$"-high gaps. The total height of the faces and gaps is 30", which should equal the standard full-

PHOTO CREDIT: CANAC KITCHENS

height door in your project.

All drawer boxes, with the exception of the top box, are 2" less in height than their drawer faces; the top box is 3" less in height than its drawer face. This cabinet requires two $8\frac{15}{16}$"-high lower drawer boxes

and one 5"-high top drawer box. The lower box is installed tightly against the bottom board and the boxes need a 2" vertical space between each other. The top box is set 1" below the lower edge of the top rail.

99

Baltic Birch Plywood Drawers

Half-inch-thick Baltic birch plywood is the favored material of many cabinetmakers for building drawer boxes. The drawer parts can be joined in a number of ways, but I'll explain the simplest method using rabbet butt joints and brad nails.

Baltic birch is also a good material to use when building pullout drawers behind doors. It's light, and the void-free edges can be sanded and finished.

Each side board has a ¼"-deep by ½"-wide rabbet on both ends to accept the front and back boards. The rabbets can be cut with a dado blade on your table saw or on a router table. The rabbet depth equals one-half the board's thickness.

The drawers are assembled using glue and brad nails. Apply glue to the rabbet cuts and attach the side boards to the front and back boards. The bottom is also attached with glue and brads.

Install the drawer-glide hardware following the manufacturer's instructions. Most slide hardware, as mentioned earlier, needs ½" clearance on each side of the drawer box. For this application I used side-mount full-extension (FX) glides, but a standard three-quarter extension glide will work just as well.

Finger-Jointed Solid-Wood Drawer Boxes

Here's a variation of a solid-wood drawer box that can be built with finger joints. The bottom $\frac{1}{4}$" panel is nailed and glued on the bottom edge of the side, front and back boards. Another style of solid-wood box, with the bottom in a groove, is shown below.

This drawer box, or tray, tracks on wood runners in grooves cut along the side boards. The drawers can also be installed using conventional drawer glides, but there must be a $\frac{1}{2}$" space on each side as explained earlier in this chapter.

The trays are $\frac{1}{16}$" narrower than the cabinet's inside width. The sides, back and front boards are $\frac{3}{4}$" hardwood stock. I will describe the process used to make finger joints for the corner joinery in the Shop Talk that follows this section, but many other joints can be used. If you decide to use a screw-and-butt joint, don't place the screws in the middle of the side boards because grooves will be cut in the center.

Cut the parts to size, then set up your $\frac{1}{2}$" finger-cutting jig (see the Shop Talk on the next page). Each finger and slot for these joints is $\frac{1}{2}$" wide. To properly interlock, the sides are indexed differently from the front and back boards. Remember to orient the boards properly when cutting each end. To guarantee correct positioning, place a mark on the bottom edges of the tray boards. Now, start all the cuts on both ends of each board with the mark facing the fixed pin.

Assemble the four trays with glue applied to all fingers and slots. Clamp the trays and measure the diagonals to ensure that they are square. If the measurements are different, a slight twist or tap on the long side should equalize the measurements.

To achieve as much drawer depth as possible, glue and nail $\frac{1}{4}$"-thick veneer plywood to the tray frame bottoms. A $\frac{3}{4}$"-wide groove is needed on both sides of each tray. They will fit over solid-wood tray runners and should be centered on each side.

The best tool to cut these grooves is a stacked dado blade on a table saw. Begin with a $\frac{1}{4}$"-deep groove on each side and test-fit the tray. If necessary, cut the grooves a little deeper to achieve the correct fit. The tray should be snug on the slides, without binding; they can be fine-tuned with sandpaper and waxed until they slide smoothly.

SHOP TALK *Building a Finger-Joint Jig*

Cutting finger or box joints is an easy procedure using your table saw, dado blade, and this shop-made jig. You'll get perfect results every time and you won't hesitate to show these joints on your projects.

Finger joints aren't restricted to drawer-box construction. They can be used in dozens of woodworking applications, including jewel or display boxes, picture frames or chests. Take your time making this jig because you'll be using it often.

1 Attach a long 1x2 board extension on your table-saw miter fence. It will be used to support the finger-joint indexing panel.

2 Clamp an indexing panel, which is about 8" high and 24" long, to the extension board on your miter fence. This tall indexing panel will help support large boards as they are pushed through the dado blade. Once it is secured, cut through the indexing panel. I am setting up and testing this jig with a ½"-wide dado blade.

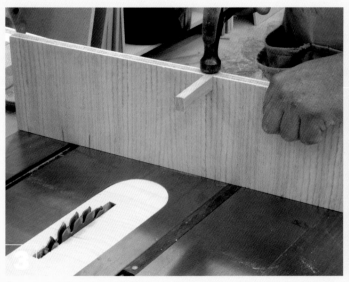

Cut a wood indexing pin that equals the cut width, then glue it in the notch on the panel.

Use a loose indexing pin, also the same width as the notch, to set the fixed indexing pin ½" away from the dado blade. Clamp the indexing board securely to the miter-fence extension.

Cut the two boards to be joined together. Hold the rear board tightly to the fixed indexing pin and set the front board away from the fixed pin using the loose spacer block as a guide. Remove the loose index pin and make the first cut.

Make the second cut with the rear board notch over the index pin and the front board held tightly to the pin. Make the remaining cuts by moving the notches over the pin until all fingers and slots have been formed.

If the test joint is loose, move the indexing panel so the fixed pin is slightly farther away from the blade. If the fingers are too wide for the notches, move the fixed indexing pin towards the blade. Be careful when moving the index board because it doesn't take very much pin movement toward or away from the blade to dramatically change the finger and slot width.

Conventional Wood Drawers

The drawer-box construction standard, before the introduction of modern materials and hardware, was a box with solid-wood sides, front and back boards. Rabbet joints were used on the corners and a $\frac{1}{4}$"-wide groove was cut in the front and side boards. The back board was reduced in height to accept a $\frac{1}{4}$"-thick plywood bottom that would overlay the back edge.

The bottom board was inset because the side-board's bottom edges tracked on wood runners. With the inset bottom, only the side edges would be in contact with the runners to reduce friction. The wood parts that contacted each other would have a coat of wax applied to reduce drag.

Many cabinetmakers still build that style of drawer today. However, an inset bottom isn't necessary any longer because drawer boxes track on modern ball-bearing and nylon drawer-glide sets. If you plan to build cabinets to match older-styled cabinets, you may want to use the inset-bottom and wood-runner combination.

1 This sample drawer box is 9" deep by 28$\frac{1}{2}$" wide. The depth is 3" at the front face. Use a dado or a standard blade on the table saw to form a $\frac{3}{8}$"-deep by $\frac{3}{4}$"-wide rabbet cut on each end of the drawer-front's back face. If the front will be covered with a drawer face, cut the rabbets in the side boards so the ends of the joints will be hidden. I cut the front and back boards for this application because I won't be adding a drawer face on this box.

2 The two side boards and the front all need a $\frac{1}{4}$"-wide by $\frac{3}{8}$"-deep groove on the inside face to receive the bottom board. This groove begins $\frac{1}{4}$" above the bottom edge of each board.

3

4

Apply glue to the front-board rabbets and attach the sides with 1"-long brass screws or finishing nails. The grooves on the sides and front board must align to receive the bottom board.

The drawer's back is $2\frac{1}{2}$" high so the $\frac{1}{4}$"-thick bottom board can be attached to its bottom edge. Attach the back board to the side board ends with glue and $1\frac{1}{2}$"-long screws. Slide the bottom panel into the grooves and secure it in place with a few brad nails driven into the back board. Or, you can use a rabbet joint on the back corners if desired.

5

Drawer glides are simple, small strips of wood that are glued and screwed to the cabinet's sides. Locate the glides so there is $\frac{1}{16}$" clearance above the drawer box. If you are building a bank of multiple drawer boxes, each with an attached drawer face, leave 1" vertical space between boxes. The faces are applied so there's a $\frac{1}{16}$" gap between them for frameless cabinets, or wider spaces for face-frame-cabinet drawer faces. Face-frame cabinets can be spaced more widely because there's a rail to cover the gap.

Locking Rabbet Drawer Joinery

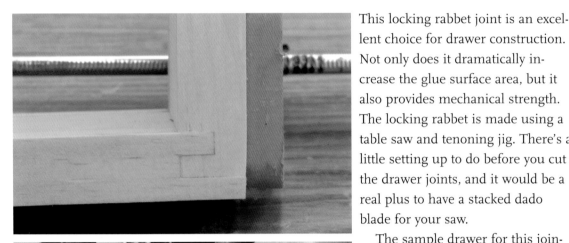

This locking rabbet joint is an excellent choice for drawer construction. Not only does it dramatically increase the glue surface area, but it also provides mechanical strength. The locking rabbet is made using a table saw and tenoning jig. There's a little setting up to do before you cut the drawer joints, and it would be a real plus to have a stacked dado blade for your saw.

The sample drawer for this joinery project will be $3\frac{1}{2}$" high by 8" wide by $22\frac{1}{2}$" long. I'm using solid pine with a $1\frac{1}{2}$"-thick veneer plywood bottom board.

1

Cut a groove in both ends of the drawer's back and front boards that's $\frac{1}{4}$" wide and $\frac{3}{4}$" deep. Center the groove using a tenoning jig and stacked dado blade.

2

Remove $\frac{3}{8}$" from one side of the material forming the groove. Complete this step for both front and back boards at each end. Be sure to remove material on the same face of each board.

3

Form a dado on the inside face of each side board that's $\frac{3}{8}$" deep and $\frac{1}{4}$" away from each end. Notice that I'm using a backer board for many of these cuts to prevent tear-out of my drawer boards as I finish the cuts.

Cut a groove for the bottom board in the two sides and front board. The groove begins ¼" above the bottom edges of the boards and is ⅜" deep.

Trim the bottom edge of the back board by ½", making it 3" high.

Assemble the drawer box with glue and clamps. The bottom ¼"-thick plywood panel is 7½" wide by 22⅛" long. It slides into the grooves and overlays the back board's bottom edge. Don't glue this panel in place; it's held with brad nails, as illustrated.

Dado-and-Rabbet Drawer Joinery

This combination joint uses a rabbet and dado to form a strong bond between the drawer's sides, front and back. The goal is to maximize surface area, which creates a stronger bond between the two parts when glue is applied. The $\frac{3}{4}$" surface area of a butt joint is doubled; when multiplied by the board's length, the board-to-board contact area increases dramatically. Clamp the joint assembly until the glue sets up.

1

The dado is $\frac{3}{8}$" deep and $\frac{1}{4}$" wide, with its back edge set $\frac{3}{4}$" from the board's edge. This joint is easily cut with a stacked dado blade on a table saw.

2

The rabbet is $\frac{1}{2}$" deep and $\frac{3}{8}$" long. It also is easily formed with a stacked dado blade on a table saw. Both cuts can also be made on a router table with a $\frac{1}{4}$"-diameter router bit.

Pocket Hole Joinery

Pocket hole joinery is now the accepted standard in many cabinet shops. It's a common joint to use when building cabinet face frames. Drawers are often assembled using pocket holes as well, but there are many other applications for this strong joinery option. My book, *The Pocket Hole Drilling Jig Project Book*, published by Popular Woodworking Books, provides an in-depth look at many other uses for this joint.

Use one of the many pocket hole drilling jigs that are available to drill the angled step holes in one of the boards to be joined. A stop collar on the step drill controls the depth, and metal guides align the holes. I prefer a square-bottom brad-point-style drill bit for this application.

Apply glue to the pieces being joined and clamp tightly. The best clamp to use is a pair of locking pliers with a round, flat holding plate. This clamp aligns the parts and holds them securely while screws are driven to secure the joint. Note that there are special screws that have a flat pan-head and thread arrangement for pocket hole joinery. In addition, there are pan-head pocket hole screws designed for soft and hard wood. Be sure to use the right combination of screw thread style and length to achieve the strongest joint possible. Most pocket hole drilling jig manufacturers provide instructions on screw selection, as do fastener suppliers.

Biscuit Joinery Options

Biscuit joinery has gained a great deal of popularity in the last ten years even though it has been in use for decades. Biscuits have replaced dowels as the hidden joinery option for cabinet construction.

Biscuits are wood wafers that fit into slots cut with a plate joiner. These wafers absorb water-based glue and expand to lock two pieces of wood together. It's an amazingly strong joint that's almost impossible to separate once the adhesive sets. Biscuit joinery is ideally suited for drawer-box construction.

1 The first step is to draw alignment lines on the two pieces being joined. The marks should be on the faces that will be aligned to each other as a reference point for the plate cutter.

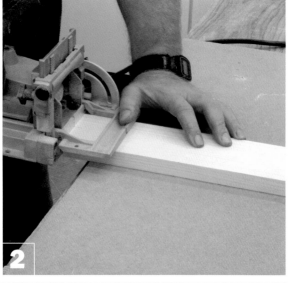

2 Set the guide plate to half the board thickness and cut a slot in the first board. You should align the plate-joiner index mark with the alignment mark on the work piece. Notice that the plate-joiner guide rests directly on the work piece and not on the work table. This will ensure that the two boards will be properly aligned at the marked surfaces.

SHOP TIP

You can learn more about the uses, procedures and benefits of biscuit joinery in a book by Popular Woodworking Books author Jim Stack titled, The Biscuit Joiner Project Book.

3 Cut the biscuit slot in the second piece to be joined. When the work piece is too narrow to properly support the joiner's guide plate, clamp a support parallel with the top edge of the board, as shown. Once again, be sure the guide plate on the cutter is aligned with the indicator mark and the plate is resting on the work piece. Cut the slot, apply glue to both surfaces as well as in the slots, and insert a biscuit. Use clamps to secure the two pieces until the adhesive sets up.

Hand-Cut Dovetails for Drawer-Box Joinery

Use a marking gauge to inscribe lines on both faces of each board. The gauge should be set at a distance equal to the board's thickness.

This traditional joinery method has been in use for decades. Fine furniture, both antique and modern versions, have always been associated with hand-cut dovetail joinery. It's one of the strongest woodworking joints available because it has mechanical strength as well as a large surface area for adhesives.

Hand-cutting dovetails takes practice, but you can easily master this joint in a short time with a little patience. There are many ways to cut dovetails. I'll illustrate one method that doesn't require any special alignment tools. In fact, measurements are not taken and guides are not used to make the joint shown here.

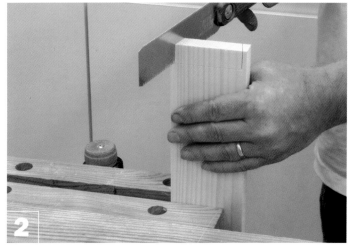

Cut the pins first. One half pin at both ends of the board is required. The angle is about 10° and the widest part of the half pin is about one-half the board's thickness. The angle cut and pin size aren't that critical because this pin board will become the template to cut the matching tail board. Be sure to cut level and straight down to the marking gauge line on each side of the board.

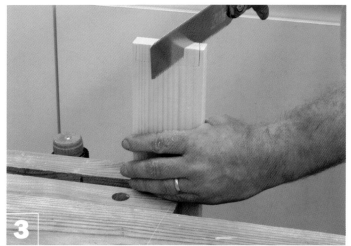

Cut the first tail space along a line opposite to the half-pin cut. The widest part of the tail space will be approximately equal to the board's thickness. Cut straight down to the marking gauge lines.

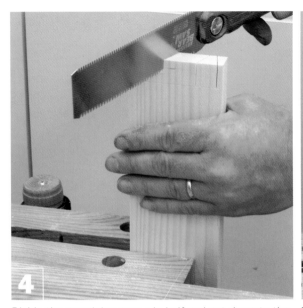

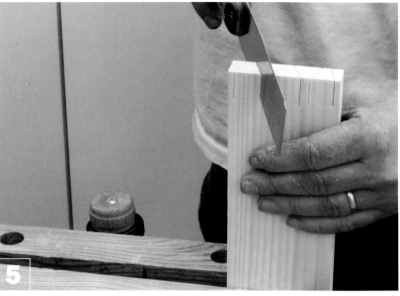

Divide the remaining space in half and cut down to the lines at the same angle as the previous cut.

Turn the saw to the same angle as the first half-pin cut. Divide the remaining spaces in half and cut down to the lines. These two cuts will form half pins, full pins, and full tails. Repeat the steps for wider boards. The final number of pins and tails will depend on the width of the boards to be joined.

Chisel out the tail spaces by first cutting along the lines with a sharp chisel.

Chisel halfway through the tail spaces. Turn the board over and chisel the remaining halfway through the board, then carefully remove the waste.

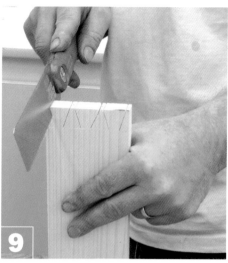

8 Use the pin board as a template to mark the tails. Mark the waste area to be removed with an X after tracing the pin outline on the tail board.

9 Cut the tail lines, being careful at this point to follow the lines. Keep the saw running accurately along the lines on the waste side of each cut.

10 Remove the half-pin waste area by cutting straight to the previously cut lines. Repeat the step on each side.

11

Cut along the marking gauge lines with a chisel and begin removing the waste. Material cannot be forced forward because of the taper on the tails, so cut through from each side and remove the waste material by pushing it out one side. Test-fit the joint and fine-tune with a file if necessary. Apply glue, assemble the joint, and clamp until the adhesive sets.

MACHINE-MADE DOVETAILS

For those woodworkers who like using dovetail joinery but prefer a machine method, there are dozens of options available. The marketplace has plenty of machine offerings at a variety of prices. A router and dovetail bit are used to follow a pattern of slotted guides to form the dovetail pins and tails.

All dovetail-cutting jigs come with detailed instructions and some also provide a video about using the jig. Each machine is slightly different, so a general explanation isn't possible. However, there are a number of excellent jigs that will allow you to make perfect dovetails for all your drawer-joinery requirements.

Inlaid Door and Drawer Faces

Inlaid doors are unique and visually attractive, particularly when contrasting species of wood are used. In this chapter, I'll use solid oak panels with walnut inlays to create these beautiful but easy-to-make cabinet doors and drawer faces.

Many types of jigs and guide systems can be used to make inlaid patterns, but I think you'll be pleased at the consistent results you can achieve by using my pattern-routing jig (described in chapter three). All sizes of door and drawer faces can be clamped in the jig, allowing you complete control of the cutting process. The jig also sets the fixed distance of the cuts from the panel's edges. This is an important point when building multiple doors, using different-sized panels, or for a project that requires more than one door size. The pattern's interior width and height changes as the door size changes,

but the distance from the edges remains constant, making all the door and drawer panels visually consistent.

Look at the photo of the three doors above. You'll notice that some of the inlaid wood is lighter in color — that's sap wood, which often is lighter than the heartwood in most trees. It was an experi-

ment on my part to see the effect of using varied wood colors for the inlay material. There's a striking difference between the inlay color on the left door (mixed heart- and sapwood) and the darker heartwood inlays in the center and right side door. Remember to consider such differences when you select your inlay wood.

Making Inlay Doors

Solid-wood glue-ups are used for this process. If you are not familiar with the steps required to create the panels, refer to the Shop Talk in chapter five, Creating Panel Glue-Ups. The pattern-routing jig described in chapter three is used to secure the panels and a plunge router, with a ¾" diameter bit for this first example door, is used to cut a groove pattern that's ⅛" deep.

Rip strips of inlay wood that are ¾" wide by 3⁄16" thick. Cutting these small pieces can be dangerous, so build the thin-strip pushing jig that is described in chapter eight. Cut as many pieces as required to fill the inlay grooves.

Cut the strips of wood to the correct length. The rounded corners of the grooves on the door panel can be squared with a chisel or they may be left round with the strips sanded to fit. I sanded the strip corners to fit the groove radius, but either method is fine.

Dry fit the inlay strips and sand, if necessary, to achieve the tightest fit possible.

Apply glue in the grooves and lightly tap the strips to seat them.

Use a heavy weight (a fully loaded toolbox works well) on top of a flat board to hold the strips while the adhesive sets up.

Once the glue has cured, fill any voids with the appropriate color of wood filler if required.

Sand the inlaid strips and door panel until you achieve a smooth surface.

I prefer to roundover the outside door profile using a $3/8$"-radius bit to "soften" the look of my inlaid doors. You may want to leave them square or use a different router bit to edge-dress your doors. Many profile bit styles are available, so experiment with a few and pick one that suits your taste.

Inlay Material Width

I used ³/₄"-wide wood strips for the previous inlaid door example. However, any size can be used; it's a matter of personal taste, based on how you want the project to look. Wider inlays are suited to heavier-styled furniture, while thinner strips can be used for smaller and more delicate-appearing furniture pieces.

For this example, I'm using a ¹/₄"-diameter router bit with the patterning jig to cut the grooves in a solid-wood door panel.

Follow the same steps, as previously detailed, of rounding the corners and fitting the strips. Dry fit all the strips, apply glue, cover with weights, and let the adhesive set up. Finish the inlay work following the above steps.

Curved inlaid patterns also can be made by adding a template in the patterning jig. The router will follow any pattern and the inlay strips can be cut to fit. If you have access to a steam bender, the inlay strips can be formed using that process. If not, you can cut the strips on a band saw from wider stock and fit them into the curve as I did.

SHOP TIP

If you decide to curve the top strip as I did, you'll have to account for the pattern position change. The template I prepared is 1" high at its center point, which means that the pattern head will be lowered by 1" on the panel. To center the panel and still leave the same space at the bottom of the inlaid pattern, I placed a board equal to the template height at center, which is 1" in this example. The top center of the pattern is lowered 1", so to balance my inlaid pattern on the door panel I must raise the bottom strip by 1".

There are dozens of pattern combinations that can be created using this jig. Use small wood arcs in the corners and you'll create convex corners. Wood inserts cut on an angle at 45° or 22$\frac{1}{2}$° in the corners will form angled corners on the pattern. The possibilities are endless; dozens of different patterns can be formed.

Tips for Building Doors and Drawers

This chapter is about one-of-a-kind issues and good-to-know details. I'll review some of the material already presented and add a few items that could be of use when building doors and drawers.

The image above is a good example of a "good-to-know" detail. Remember to check the "square" of doors and drawers after assembly and before the glue sets up. If the diagonal measurements equal each other, the door or drawer box is square. If the measurements are not equal, adjust the project by shortening the long side before the glue sets up. Do this by loosening the clamps and moving one end of each clamp sideways (about $^1/_4$" at a time) towards the short diagonal corner. Then retighten the clamps. Recheck the diagonal measurements. Keep making adjustments to the clamps until the diagonal measurements are equal.

Shop-Made Router-Table Fence

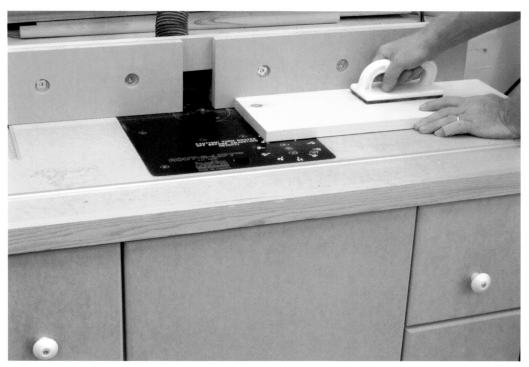

Throughout this book I've been working with a router table. A few of the milling operations can be dangerous, so safety is the number-one concern. It occurred to me that many woodworkers do not have a good adjustable router fence for their table. Free-cutting a piece of wood guided only by the router-bit bearing isn't wise, so I always use a fence. The fence is a safety backup that also can be used in partnership with the router-bit bearing as a guide system.

The fence can prevent the work piece from being driven behind the router bit, which could result in an injury. My advice is to buy a good fence or spend a few dollars and build the one shown here. This one has adjustable face plates to minimize the bit exposure and maximize safety.

1

All of the fence parts are made with ³⁄₄"-thick MDF. The upright fence board is 5" high by 39" long and the horizontal fence board is 4" high by 39" long, but those dimensions can be altered to suit your table. The upright rail has two ³⁄₈"-wide grooves routed into the center and through the board. The grooves start 6" from each end and stop 16" from each end. This rail also requires a 4"-wide by 2¹⁄₂"-high notch, centered on the length of the board. The horizontal board also has a center notch that is 4" wide by 2" high. Both notches can be cut with a band saw or jig saw.

Attach the vertical fence board to the horizontal board with glue and 1½"-long screws installed approximately 6" on center. Remember to drill pilot holes before driving the screws to avoid material splits.

The four right-angle fence supports are 4"x4" blocks of ¾" MDF cut at 45°. Use glue and 1½"-long screws to attach the supports to the fence assembly. Install one support at each end, and the remaining two on each side of the cut-out notch in the fence boards.

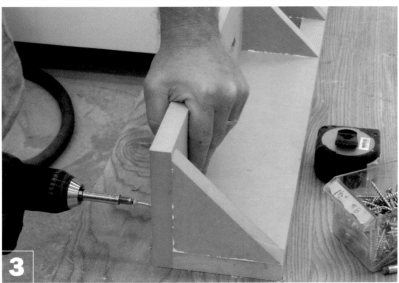

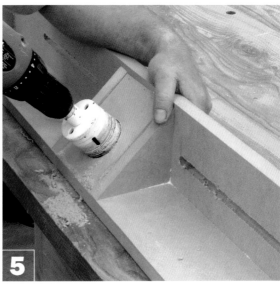

The back cover for the fence cutout has a 45° miter on both ends. Apply glue to all edges and secure the cover with a few brad nails on the top and bottom edges.

Drill a 2¼"-diameter hole in the center of the back cover. This will be used to friction-fit a vacuum hose.

SHOP TIP

T-tracks, knobs, nuts and other related hardware are available at your local woodworking store. There is usually a wide selection of hardware that can be used to make all kinds of shop jigs or workstations. More than ten workshop stations you can make for your shop that use this type of hardware are described in my book, **Building Woodshop Workstations.**

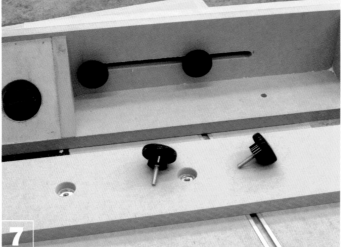

The T-track, which will be used to lock the adjustable fence, can be attached to the router tabletop in grooves. Rout the grooves on each side parallel to your router plate, matching the depth of track you purchased and making sure they are flush with the tabletop surface. Once again, the tracks are secured with $\frac{5}{8}$"-long screws. Center the fence assembly on the router table and drill two $\frac{3}{8}$"-diameter holes in the horizontal support over the center of each T-track. Use a T-slot nut and knob with a 1"-long by $\frac{1}{4}$"-diameter threaded shaft screwed into the nut. Tighten the knobs and verify that the fence locks securely.

The two adjustable fence boards have two three-prong T-nuts driven into the front faces. Counterbore the holes so the nuts are below the fence faces. Position the nuts so both fences can come together in the center and travel about 4" out from the center of the fence cutout.

The $2\frac{1}{4}$" outer diameter hose on my shop vacuum fits snugly in the dust hole and provides good particle removal.

INSTALLING DRAWER FACES

Drawer faces can be accurately installed by first drilling holes for the handles or knobs. Drill holes in the drawer faces only, not the drawer box at this point. Hold the bottom-drawer face in place, flush with the lower edge of the bottom board and equally spaced on the cabinet's side edges or stiles on a face-frame cabinet, then drive $1\frac{1}{2}$"-long screws into the drawer box through the handle holes. The drawer face is now securely anchored to the box in the proper position and screws can be driven through the drawer box into the back of the drawer face.

Next, place a $\frac{1}{16}$"-thick spacer (or whatever width is required) between the bottom and middle drawer faces. Repeat the steps for the middle and top faces. Once the drawer faces are secured, handles can be attached by removing the temporary screws in the handle holes, drilling through the drawer box, and using machine screws to mount the handles.

PULLOUTS BEHIND CABINET DOORS

Pullouts are often installed behind a full-height cabinet door. Normally, pullouts and drawer boxes using most drawer-glide hardware are 1" narrower than the cabinet's inside width. However, pullouts behind doors need extra clearance to travel past the door. Hidden hinges (European hinges) open within their own width but do enter the inside cabinet space when opened. A spacer cleat must be installed on the hinge side(s). If the base cabinet has one door with hinge plates attached to the left side panel, you will need one spacer cleat on the left for each pullout. The cleats are $\frac{5}{8}$"-thick melamine PB with all visible edges covered with tape. They are secured to the side panel using 1"-long PB screws in piloted countersunk holes.

DRAWER-BOX ALIGNMENT

Drawer boxes installed on standard three-quarter extension glides must seat properly on both runners. The following procedure will allow you to get more consistent results when using these glide systems.

Use a carpenter's square to draw a screw hole guide line at a 90° angle to the cabinet's front edge. Be sure the cabinet's runners are installed parallel and that both are the same distance from the cabinet's bottom board. Install one screw in the front, and one in the middle of the slotted hole at the back end of each runner. The cabinet glide member's front edge should be $\frac{1}{8}$" behind the cabinet's front-face edge.

Attach the drawer-box runners with four screws and install the drawer box. Test each front corner by pressing down on the box. If either corner moves down, the rear end of the glide is higher than it should be and must be lowered. Test the corners again until there's no downward deflection of the box.

DOOR AND DRAWER HANDLE PLACEMENT

I'm often asked where to place door and drawer handles. There isn't a set standard, but I, like many other cabinetmakers, have a personal preference for placement.

I believe the handles should be placed where they are the most functional. That's the reason I always install one handle or knob at the center of a drawer face. Most people open drawers with only one hand; so if you have a knob on each side of the drawer typically only one will be used, resulting in unnecessary twisting of the drawer box. One handle in the center means the pull force will always be divided equally over both drawer runners.

As far as handle or knob placement on doors is concerned, I once again look at the practical side of

things. My door handles are typically located in the lower corner opposite the hinges on upper cabinets, and on the upper corner for base-cabinet doors. I try to install handles in the most convenient location on tall cab-

inets and apply the same logic to all of my other cabinet doors and drawer projects. You may have different considerations for placing your handles; it's up to you to decide the best location for each project.

INSIDE WIDTH PLUS 1"

When using hidden hinges, remember the 1" rule for calculating the door width. Measure the inside cabinet width and add 1"; that's the required door width. If you need two doors, divide the inside dimension plus 1" by two.

Do not base the door-width calculation on outside cabinet dimensions. A 12"-wide cabinet built with $5/8$"-thick material requires an $11^3/4$"-wide door. The same 12"-wide cabinet built with $3/4$"-thick material needs an $11^1/2$"-wide door. Hinge mechanics are based on a fixed overlay that remains constant no matter how thick the carcass material is.

FACE-FRAME DRAWER-BOX SIZE

Drawer-box sizes for face-frame cabinets installed on standard bottom-mount glides are easily determined using the 1" rule. The box is 1" less in width than the cabinet's interior width. It is also 1" less in height than the drawer-box opening's height.

Frameless-cabinet drawer-box sizes are a bit more complicated to determine. You can follow the easy formula outlined in chapter nine.

SCREW JOINERY

Make this a golden rule when using screws: Never drive a screw without drilling a pilot hole. The screw shaft is a geometric wedge that serves only to hold the thread in place. It must displace material when installed, so if you provide an empty space for the shaft, there will be a lot less material splitting. In addition, try to keep screws 1" away from panel ends to further increase your success with screw joinery.

SUPPLIERS

Many suppliers have contributed products, material and technical support during the project-building phase of this book. I appreciate how helpful they've been and recommend these companies without hesitation. If you have trouble locating a product that I've mentioned, please e-mail me at danny@cabinetmaking.com.

ADAMS & KENNEDY — THE WOOD SOURCE
6178 Mitch Owen Road
P.O. Box 700
Manotick, Ontario
Canada K4M 1A6
613-822-6800
www.wood-source.com
Wood supply

ADJUSTABLE CLAMP COMPANY
417 North Ashland Avenue
Chicago, Illinois 60622
312-666-0640
www.adjustableclamp.com
Clamps and woodworking tools

DELTA MACHINERY
4825 Highway 45 North
P.O. Box 2468
Jackson, Tennessee 38302-2468
800-223-7278 (U.S.)
800-463-3582 (Canada)
www.deltawoodworking.com
Woodworking tools

EXAKTOR TOOLS, LTD.
136 Watline #182
Mississaugua, Ontario
Canada L4C 2E2
800-387-9789
www.exaktortools.com
Sliding tables and other accessories for the table saw

GENERAL AND GENERAL INTERNATIONAL
8360, du Champ-d'Eau
Montreal, Quebec
Canada H1P 1Y3
514-326-1161
www.general.ca
Woodworking machinery

HOUSE OF TOOLS LTD.
100 Mayfield Common Northwest
Edmonton, Alberta
Canada T5P 4B3
800-661-3987
www.houseoftools.com
Woodworking tools and hardware

JESSEM TOOL COMPANY
124 Big Bay Point Road
Barrie, Ontario
Canada L4N 9B4
866-272-7492
www.jessem.com
Rout-R-Slide and Rout-R-Lift

LRH ENTERPRISES, INC.
9250 Independence Avenue
Chatsworth, California 91311
800-423-2544 (U.S.)
818-782-0226 (outside U.S.)
www.lrhent.com
Router bits and the Magic Molder

LANGEVIN & FOREST
9995 Pie IX Boulevard
Montreal, Quebec
Canada H1Z 3X1
800-889-2060
www.langevinforest.com
Tools, hardware and lumber

LEE VALLEY TOOLS LTD.
P.O. Box 1780
Ogdensburg, New York 13669-6780
800-871-8158 (U.S.)
800-267-8767 (Canada)
www.leevalley.com
Woodworking tools and hardware

PORTER-CABLE
4825 Highway 45 North
P.O. Box 2468
Jackson, Tennessee 38302-2468
800-321-9443
www.porter-cable.com
Woodworking tools

RICHELIEU HARDWARE
7900, West Henri-Bourassa
Ville St-Laurent, Quebec
Canada H4S 1V4
800-619-5446 (U.S.)
800-361-6000 (Canada)
www.richelieu.com
Hardware supplies

ROCKLER WOODWORKING AND HARDWARE
4365 Willow Drive
Medina, Minnesota 55340
800-279-4441
www.rockler.com
Woodworking tools and hardware

TREND MACHINERY & CUTTING TOOLS LTD.
Odhams Trading Estate
St. Albans Road
Watford
Hertfordshire, U.K.
WD24 7TR
01923 224657
www.trendmachinery.co.uk
Woodworking tools and hardware

VAUGHAN & BUSHNELL MFG. CO.
11414 Maple Avenue
Hebron, Illinois 60034
815-648-2446
www.vaughanmfg.com
Hammers and other tools

WOLFCRAFT NORTH AMERICA
333 Swift Road
Addison, Illinois 60601-1448
630-773-4777
www.wolfcraft.com
Woodworking hardware

WOODCRAFT
P.O. Box 1686
Parkersburg, West Virginia 26102-1686
800-535-4482
www.woodcraft.com
Woodworking hardware

WOODWORKER'S HARDWARE
P.O. Box 180
Sauk Rapids, Minnesota 56379-0180
800-383-0130
www.wwhardware.com
Woodworking hardware

**PLYWOOD AND PARTICLEBOARD MATERIAL
INFORMATION AND SUPPLIERS**
www.panolam.com
www.uniboard.com

INDEX